THE HAMLYN ENCYCLOPEDIA OF
DECORATIVE
TECHNIQUES

THE HAMLYN ENCYCLOPEDIA OF
DECORATIVE
TECHNIQUES

in association with
The Rome Academy of Decorative Arts

HAMLYN

Acknowledgements:
Isabella Caldarola, Angela Colamarco, Gina De Bellis,
Giovannella D'Amico, Vaga Ferracini, Mariange Grabau,
Sveva Groppello, Daniela Latini, Susanna Montagna, Piero
Pietracci, Marisa Rossi, Federica Tedesco, Lisa Voghel and
"Cose di non solo pane"

Special thanks to Emanuela Bongianni and Daniela
Urbinati for their assistance in taking the photographs.

First published in the United Kingdom in 1997 by
Hamlyn
an imprint of Reed International Books Ltd
Michelin House, 81 Fulham Road, London, SW3 6RB
and Auckland, Melbourne, Singapore and Toronto

Copyright © 1995 Arnoldo Mondadori Editore S.p.A., Milan

Photography by Gianni Buocanni
Jacket design by Senate
English translation by Peter Eustace, CSA snc, Verona, Italy

A CIP record for this book is available from the British Library

ISBN 0 600 59151 4

The publishers have made every effort to ensure that all
instructions given in this book are accurate and safe, but they
cannot accept liability for any resulting injury, damage or loss
to either person or property whether direct or consequential
and howsoever arising. The publishers will be grateful for any
information which will assist them in keeping future editions
up to date.

Printed and bound in Spain
D.L. TO: 1052-1996

CONTENTS

6   *INTRODUCTION*

9   TOOLS AND COLOURS

13   Using colours

**17   PREPARING
        SURFACES**

28   Base decoration
40   Finishing

45   ORNAMENTAL DECORATION

50   Décor

57   IMITATION MARBLE

60   "Peperino" and "Pietra Serena"
61   Red porphyry
62   Travertine
63   "Lumachella carnacina"
64   Lapis Lazuli
66   Alabaster
68   St. Denis green
69   Aver green
70   "Serpentina moschinata"
71   Sienna yellow
73   Marquina black
74   Antique green "breccia"
76   Malachite

79   IMITATION WOOD

82   Walnut
84   Mahogany

86   Palissander
88   Briar
91   Fir

97   STENCILS

100   Stencils on wood
104   Stencils on fabric

107   RUSTIC PAINTING

110   Country décor
116   Tyrolean décor
122   Découpage

125   GRISAILLE

131   THE GROTESQUE

133   Grotesque on wood
136   Grotesque on walls

141   TROMPE L'OEIL

161   Illusions of interiors
170   Illusions of exteriors

**183   GOLD
         AND SILVER WORK**

184   Gilding
187   Silvering

189   *Glossary*

INTRODUCTION

I have always been attracted to colours, from the time when I spent hours and hours in the studio where my grandfather painted his pictures. Over and above painting as such I have also always been fascinated by the possibility of modifying the environment around me: a white canvas, an old piece of furniture, a bare wall. I feel that only manual work can give free rein to one's imagination, achieving unusually immediate personal gratification. Using old and new materials in the search for that special effect; developing new methods to give painting the illusion of time gone by; restoring an old item of furniture stored in the attic for years, giving it a new breath of life; painting on a wall a dream to penetrate with both the eyes and the mind: all this should not be seen merely as a task but, especially and always, as a new and exciting game.

A meeting with Simonetta Perrone and Stefania Bonacelli gave me the chance to make on old dream come true. I set up and organized a centre where various decorative techniques could be taught and where new creative experiences could be developed. Since the creation of the *Academy of Decorative Arts*, I have become increasingly aware of the popular passion for decoration. This book is the answer to the needs of those who, unable to attend courses, want to learn the art of decoration. The aim of this book, then, is to provide readers with a tool which will help them tackle the decorative arts for the first time, learning to begin with the fundamental notions and improving manual skills, proceeding subsequently towards more difficult and complex projects. The first part of the book, therefore, has an essentially educational character: it aims to provide readers with the necessary bases for decorating an object or a wall. Above all, detailed emphasis is given to the characteristics of various materials to ensure optimal selection and best use, not the least through an initial introduction to the use of colour. The book then moves onto the preparation of the surfaces to be decorated; lastly, special attention is paid to the most important finishing techniques used to protect, lacquer or antiquate finished decorations. A long section deals with the design of decorations and the realization of drawings, together with useful hints and tips aimed at making tasks easier and faster. The various stages in producing the major European decorative motifs are also presented, with special attention to the main potential mistakes and problems which can easily be avoided.

This educational introduction to decoration undoubtedly facilitates the first approach to the various techniques, each accompanied by a brief historical discussion highlighting origins and popularity. Here again, the approach is gradual, presenting these techniques in increasing order of difficulty: imitation marble, imitation wood, stencils, rustic painting, grisaille, the grotesque, trompe l'oeil, gilding and silver work.

Each of these kinds of décor is accompanied by a sequential description of the various stages involved in preparing a project, complete with detailed photographs used in the lessons held at the Academy and a number of personal works by the founder members. Every type of decoration is accompanied by a list of the materials needed, main colours and basic technical notions - such as the theory of light and shade or the main rules of perspective. A special effort was made in the chapter dealing with trompe l'oeil <u>not</u> to provide hard and fast rules and rigid procedures, since it is important to remember that the <u>main</u> gift of a decorator is undoubtedly imagination: readers will therefore be able to select the base and decoration in line with personal preferences and requirements, while still being able to make the best choices through an awareness of necessary information.

Marzia Damaggio Campos

TOOLS AND COLOURS

T he pictorial techniques described in this book do not involve an expensive outlay in purchasing materials. All you need to start off with is basic equipment essentially comprising items found in every household: newspapers, sheets of plastic used to cover tables and floors, a bucket and rags, paper towels, plastic cups, plates and spoons and disposable gloves.

These articles are joined by everything else needed to carry out the project and the design. Such materials are easy to find in stationers, ironmongers or art shops: pencils (hard), erasers and pencil-sharpeners, rulers and set-squares, tape, cutters, scissors, transfer and graphite paper, ruled paper, rollers, plumb-lines and spirit-levels. Tools needed for painting include brushes, dyes, paints and natural sponges.

Having decided precisely which decoration you want to undertake, before starting on the task you should first make sure that everything needed is ready at hand (including solvents), to avoid the risk of having to interrupt the decoration project because something is missing.

A number of things must be borne in mind before beginning. First and foremost, it is a good idea to protect the workplace with newspapers or sheets of plastic and, if possible, set up a worktable where everything needed can be placed in easy reach. If the surfaces to be painted (such as walls or wardrobes) are rather high, use a ladder/trestle or steps - but remember that some kind of receptacle will be needed where tools can be placed.

You must also be careful about clothing, since it is easy to spoil clothes beyond repair. For example, when painting vertical surfaces splashes can easily mark shoes, which can then only be thrown away, because acrylic and water-based paints - once dry - are difficult to remove because they penetrate into the fibres. Lastly, it is a good idea to keep a bucket of water and a roll of paper towels handy; they may be useful at any time, even simply to clean paint from your hands.

All this goes beyond the materials needed to treat surfaces and for lacquering, which are discussed separately.

Once the basic materials are ready (bucket, rags, paper towels, adhesive tape, glass-paper, ruler, pencil, sponge [photograph above], brushes, paints, dyes and colours, plumb-line), work can begin on any kind of decorative technique, from the simplest to the most complex.

Brushes

Together with paints, dyes and colours, brushes are vitally important in producing works of decorative art.
Use good quality brushes (to avoid the risk of spoiling the final result) of the right type, material and dimensions.
There are various kinds and sizes of brush, indicated by numbers which correspond to the format of the bristles; for example a 60 mm.
Brushes are available in sizes from 00 mm upwards (the smaller the number, the thinner the tip).
The selection of a particular brush -

Flat brushes (left) are used in imitation marble work.
To prepare and decorate bases, use wide boar bristle brushes (below).

A range of different types and sizes of brush should be available.
Flat-tipped brushes in ox bristle and retouching brushes in synthetic sable (right) are used for decoration.

more or less flexible, more or less soft - depends on the pictorial technique.
There are brushes for applying base coats, thin lines, preparation and decoration of bases, lacquer-work and finishing.
They may be in synthetic fibre, boar bristle, ox bristle, synthetic sable, with square or rounded, flat or conical tips.
A good paintbrush must have a soft tip, so preference goes to synthetic sable or ox bristle brushes.
The thickness of the bristles must be appropriate to the surface to be painted; if a large brush is used for borders or touching-up, there is the risk of straying outside the area effectively to be painted; if a large area is to be covered and the tip of the paintbrush is too

small, a single brush stroke will not cover the area properly and the final colour will seem irregular or spotted.
It is advisable, therefore, to have at least two different sizes of finishing brush ready to hand.
For lines and borders around a decoration, use bristle brushes with a flat tip of a size suitable for the line to be marked out.
When preparing and decorating base surfaces, it is best to use larger brushes in boar bristle available in various sizes: 40, 50, 60 mm and above.
Since brushes used to prepare and decorate such surfaces wear out quickly - and since high quality is not essential for these tasks - cheaper ones can be used.

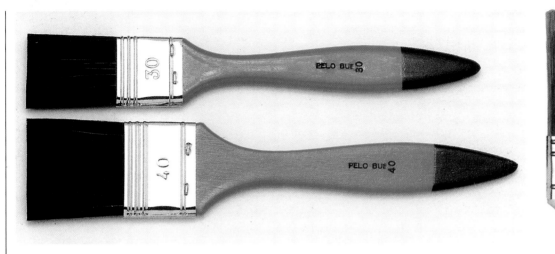

Very soft brushes should be used for lacquering, since brush strokes ought to be almost invisible. The best ones for this task are ox bristle brushes. Nylon brushes, which are much less expensive, should only be used for acrylic lacquers which, being water-dilutable, do not require the use of solvents; they should only be cleaned with soap and water. Ox bristle brushes are ideal for turpentine-based lacquers and polyurethane gels. If brushes have to be used with materials that cannot be diluted in water, they should be cleaned with specific solvents (generally indicated on the product and sold together with it). Repeated washing in a little solvent (which should be changed frequently) suffices for a clean result; the brushes should then be wiped delicately on a paper towel, washed with a little neutral soap and then rinsed in running water.

The solvents used for oil-based lacquers are genuine turpentine and spirit of turpentine; nitro and acetone solvents are used for polyurethane products. Use old or cheap brushes to apply wax or bitumen.

Never leave brushes immersed in solvent. If this is unavoidable, for example because work has to be interrupted frequently, it is a good idea to cut a hole in a piece of cardboard of such a size that, slipping the brush through the hole and placing the card over the solvent container, the brush itself does not rest on the bottom.

Special flogger brushes have truncated tips; sizes are proportional to the dimensions of the cut-outs in the stencil. Brushes should be washed at the end of each task, dried and stored carefully, taking care not to bend the tips. Store them flat or upside-down in a glass.

Top left: ox bristle brushes for lacquering. Above: nylon brush specifically for acrylic lacquers. Below: stencil brushes.

Water-based paints (above), acrylic paints (top right) and earths (right) have different features. The pictorial outcome of the decoration depends on the selection and application of specific paints.

Paints

The pictorial outcome of a decoration depends on the technique used and, consequently, on the choice of paints and dyes. The chromatic qualities of the chosen product are therefore extremely important, not to mention its elasticity, good surface adherence, resistance to scratches, heat, light and water; these features determine the ease with which the task is performed and the durability of the decoration.

Acrylic paints
The acrylic paints used in fine arts are available in a wide variety of shades, making it possible to achieve all the special effects needed for certain pictorial techniques, such as reproducing the appearance of marble. Since they can be diluted in water, solvents are not required (solvents

are toxic, harmful to health and extremely polluting).
Fine art acrylic paints provide less coverage than water-based paints and are more expensive. On the other hand, they do not yellow with age, stand up to temperature variations and, since they are porous, tend not to form bubbles. When diluted, colours become paler and more transparent like water colours.

Water-based paints
Water-based paints are available commercially in an enormous range of shades, dry rapidly and are not expensive. They provide good coverage and, if highly diluted, give excellent veiling effects. Such paints are also available for external applications, resisting bad weather, pollution and mould. Brushes last longer and are easier to clean when using water-based paints. These paints can also be mixed with acrylic paints to extend the range of colours even further; in this case, however, use high quality brands and be careful to avoid the formation of lumps when mixing the two different products.

Earths
This is the name given to certain powdery pigments, such as sienna and umber, which, with ochre and a few others, were originally the base products with which dyes could be prepared.
Earths are found in art shops in the form of coloured, natural or chemically synthetic powders; some are very expensive. Diluted in water or an acrylic bonding agent, their colours are extremely natural; they are very transparent and ideal for delicate decorations. They can be mixed together and with the addition of a little white water-based paint become more full-bodied for better coverage. They have to be protected by a finishing coat

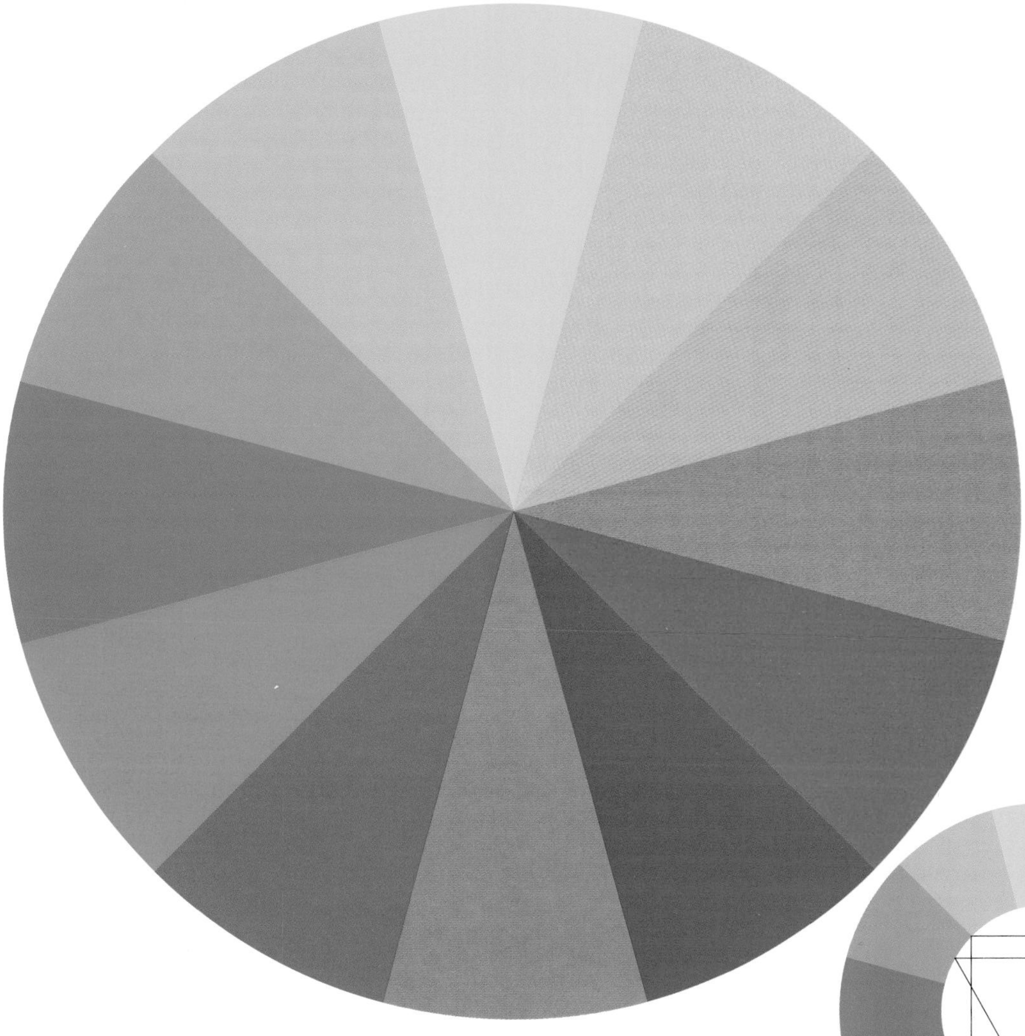

The colour disc comprises twelve colours: primary (red, yellow, blue) and secondary (orange, green, violet) produced by mixing primary colours two-by-two, plus six other colours made by mixing primary and secondary colours. The colour disc makes it easy to understand at a glance the features of a colour and its components, facilitating colour selection not the least in terms of luminosity and intensity. The triangle and square drawn inside the disc (figure below) are used to identify harmonious colours: turning them around inside the circle, three or four groups of colours are highlighted.

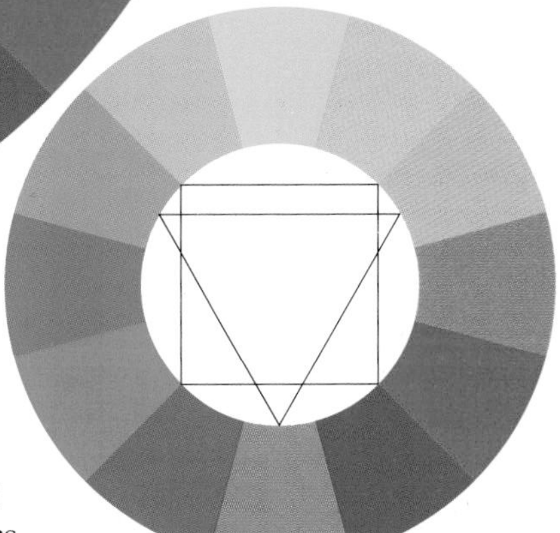

USING COLOURS

Sunlight, which seems to be white, is in fact made up of the seven colours of the spectrum: red, yellow, orange, green, blue, indigo and violet. The objects around us reflect light: a red object appears red because it absorbs all colours except red, which it reflects for us to see.

Physics has divided colours into primary colours (red, yellow, blue) and secondary colours (orange, green, violet). So, when yellow is mixed with red, orange is formed, yellow plus blue gives green and red plus blue gives violet.

The colour disc comprises twelve colours, six of which are described above and a further six are obtained by mixing primary colours again with the secondary colours derived from them. By multiplying the possible combinations, discs or charts of more than twelve colours can be made.

The colour disc gives an idea of the features of a colour at a glance, such as its components (and percentages), its complementary colours (diametrically opposite colours), whether it is a warm colour, i.e. absorbs light (from yellow to violet) or a cold colour, i.e. reflects light (green to blue). Warm and cold colours respectively lie above and below the line joining green and red.

Lemon yellow

Ochre

Red

Oxide red

Ultramarine

Blue

Emerald green

Green

Sienna

Umber

White

Black

Working with colours - i.e. mixing base colours in different proportions - considerably extends the range of shades.

For example, grey is made by mixing white and black; the shade can be made warmer by adding a little ochre or colder with a little blue.

Grey can also be prepared without using black: mix two complementary colours in equal parts and then modify the percentages until the required shade and density are achieved.

Beige is obtained by mixing umber, ochre and white. For a more pinkish effect, add a little red, or blue for a colder appearance; for more luminosity, add a little lemon yellow.

Throughout this book, reference is often made to a number of terms and expressions concerning colour; it is important to understand them. Here is a list:

- Warming a colour: add ochre or umber. Clearly, shades depend on the proportions of the various colours.

- Cooling a colour: add blue.

- Making a colour more luminous: add white.

- Darkening a colour: add black.

- Lightening a colour: a brush stroke of the same colour but of much higher luminosity (more white), added to the side of a decorative element in a "half moon" shape.

- Shadowing a colour: a brush stroke in a darker colour near to or opposite the lighter one, again with a "half moon" shape.

- Shading a colour: gradual movement from a darker to a lighter colour.

If we draw an equilateral triangle or a square inside the disc, when these are rotated the vertices easily indicate three or four harmonious colours. Placing complementary colours side-by-side, or primary and secondary colours, gives rise to distinctly different contrasts. To avoid matching errors and achieve colour harmony, simply select from the colour disc those colours which are close together; if a greater colour contrast is needed, select diametrically opposite colours. When selecting colours, it is important to bear in mind their luminosity (the higher the percentage of white, the more luminous the colour), purity and intensity (shade). As a general rule, use colours of equal intensity, since the final result of the decoration will undoubtedly be more harmonious.

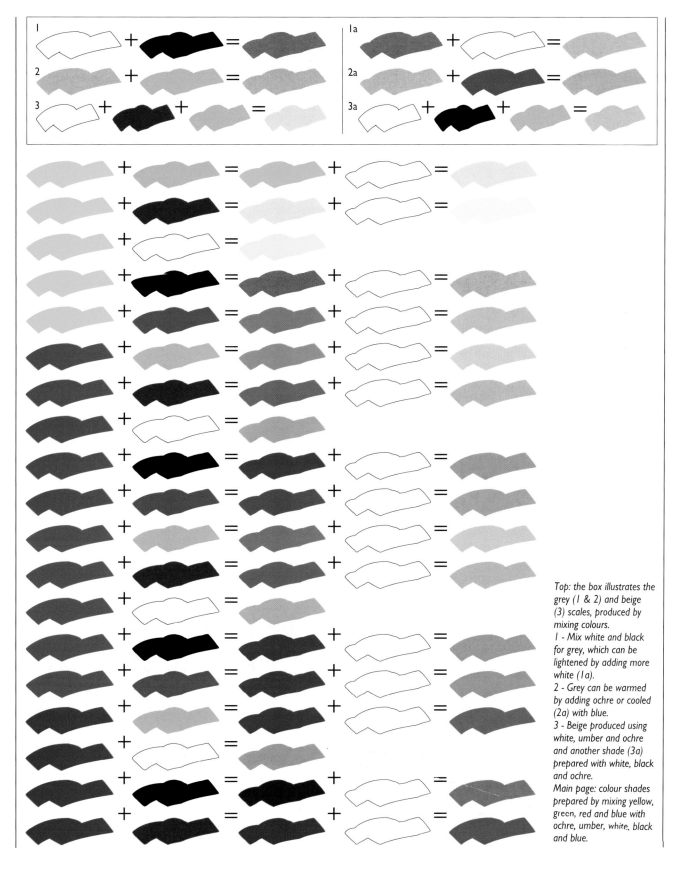

Top: the box illustrates the grey (1 & 2) and beige (3) scales, produced by mixing colours.
1 - Mix white and black for grey, which can be lightened by adding more white (1a).
2 - Grey can be warmed by adding ochre or cooled (2a) with blue.
3 - Beige produced using white, umber and ochre and another shade (3a) prepared with white, black and ochre.
Main page: colour shades prepared by mixing yellow, green, red and blue with ochre, umber, white, black and blue.

PREPARING SURFACES

A good decoration, over and above enhancement and embellishment, has to last, withstanding the normal wear and tear to which any decorated object is subjected. You may decide to decorate a wall, something in bare wood, an old piece of furniture, an earthenware vase or a gypsum column but, in each instance, you should carefully study the type of surface to define what kind of base treatment is needed. Before beginning to paint, it is essential to prepare the surface properly, since the final outcome of the decoration depends entirely on this operation. If, for example, a rough surface is not correctly polished in preparation for imitation marble decoration, imperfections will spoil the end result. Untreated bare wood is clearly porous and paint, penetrating into the fibres, makes further decoration impossible. The same thing can happen with earthenware or gesso. When starting a decoration task on a wall, pay close attention to the kind of paint with which it has already been coated, since incompatible materials compromise fixing, so that the top coat does not adhere fully. Paint may also detach from poorly prepared plaster, since it tends to form a film which, if a good bond is not achieved, gradually peels off.

Surfaces to be decorated must therefore be prepared in advance; this requires not only a good idea of the particular surface's characteristics but also those of the products you intend to use.

Many different products are available for the preparation of base surfaces, which can be diluted in water or turpentine; these products are distinguished by specific characteristics which are more or less appropriate to the decoration task in hand.

Every material has to be treated in line with its specific characteristics. Ironmongers supply everything needed for proper surface preparation treatment.

Below: a wooden screen prepared with two coats of matt water-based paint. Right: the same screen decorated with trompe l'oeil picture frames reproducing hand-painted scenes from old prints.

The materials needed to prepare base surfaces (sealing primer and water-based products), as well as to protect decorations (waxes and water-based lacquers).
Stuccos, spatulas, rubber pads, glass paper, pliers and scrapers are also needed.

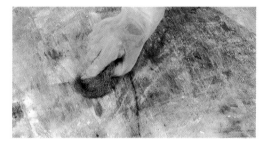

Top left: the stripper is applied thickly to the coffee table; right: as soon as the product begins to take effect, old paint is removed with a scraper. Centre: all the paint, by now dissolved in the solvent, is removed. Bottom: to eliminate residues of paint, rub the surface with steel wool or a wire brush.

Wood and fibreboard

As already mentioned, different and appropriate treatments are needed for every kind of material.

Let's begin with the initial preparation required for surfaces in wood or composite wood or compressed wood derivatives. Composite wood is much heavier than wood itself and much less expensive; it is available in DIY centres already cut into the required dimensions and thicknesses, with edges finished like slabs of marble.

When planning marble effects and a surface has to be purchased because one is not already available, it is generally preferable to buy a piece of MDF (medium density fibreboard); its surface, smoother than wood, does not need sandpapering and, since it is much less porous, requires much fewer coats of primer (a white base coating).

Paint-stripping

This is not a particularly complex operation but it has to be performed in different ways depending on whether the natural wood is protected by only one coat of clear lacquer or a surface with old paintwork.

In the first instance, it may suffice simply to sandpaper the surface until the lacquer is completely removed. If layers of old paint have to be removed to return the wood to its natural condition (thereby retaining natural veining), it is essential to paint-strip the surface. There are many commercially available paint strippers: however, all are toxic and potentially harmful to health. When using such material, take every necessary precaution. Firstly, read the instructions on the packaging, wear

protective PVC gloves and ventilate the room where work is to be carried out. The stripper must be applied only to dust- and grease-free clean surfaces. The product must penetrate well into all cracks; it should then be brushed over the smooth surfaces and dabbed into the grooves and cracks in the wood. Any kind of brush can be used, the older the better, since paint stripper ruins the bristles. If a brush has to be bought, purchase a 40-50 mm boar bristle brush since it is

HINTS AND TIPS

Having used paint stripper, it is important to remove every residual trace before preparing the surface.

not particularly expensive.

When the product has taken effect, the paint is removed with a scraper, which has to be cleaned frequently during this task. If the surface has been treated with more than one coat of paint, apply more paint stripper (but not quite such a thick layer) and when it begins to take effect start with a scraper and then steel wool (remember to change it frequently to retain abrasive power).

Stuccoing

If when the wood is finally in its natural state there are small cracks or holes, stuccoing is highly recommended. Stuccos are available as ready-to-use pastes, in a variety of colours, which must be selected in the shade closest to that of the wood to be treated.

The stucco should be softened and well amalgamated (place a little in the palm of one hand and work it with the tip of a knife, like butter); if it is too hard, a little water can be added. This paste is then used to fill the cracks in the wood; if too much is used, remove the excess.

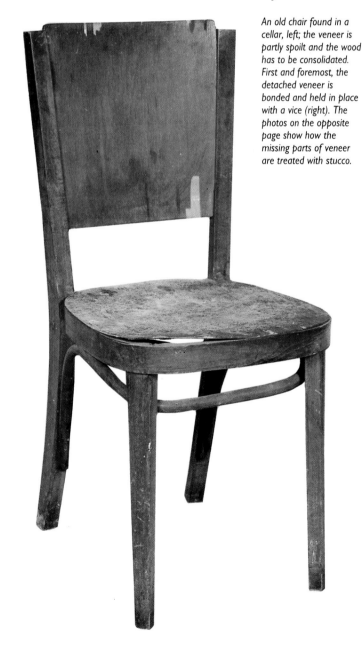

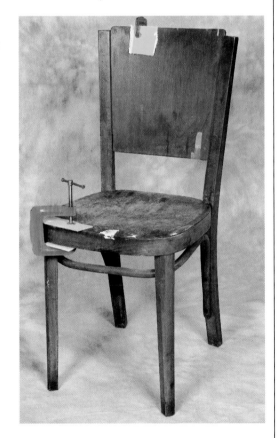

An old chair found in a cellar, left; the veneer is partly spoilt and the wood has to be consolidated. First and foremost, the detached veneer is bonded and held in place with a vice (right). The photos on the opposite page show how the missing parts of veneer are treated with stucco.

When the stucco has dried completely, use glass-paper to smooth off the surface; start with paper n. 150 and then a finer grain, such as n. 230 or n. 300. If the cracks to be filled are very deep, the stuccoing operation will have to be repeated several times.

If the wood is in very poor condition indeed, it may also be necessary - having completed stucco-work - to consolidate the veneer. To do this, use a syringe to inject vinyl glue diluted in plenty of water underneath the surface

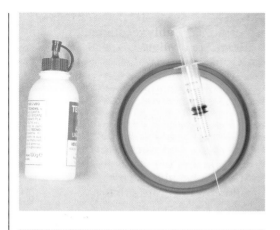

Left: vinyl glue can easily be applied to areas to be bonded with a syringe. It is important to dilute it with plenty of water.
Below: various kinds of abrasive, glass- and silicon papers.

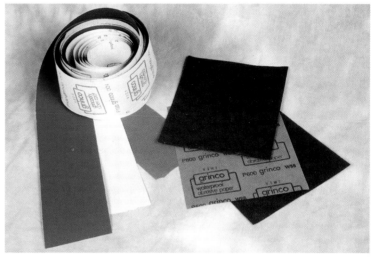

to be reattached.
The treated section must then be kept clamped in a vice for 24 hours.
If there are gaps in the veneer, these must be filled with stucco so that the overall surface is level before the base is prepared for final decoration.
It is important that this "repair" technique for wood (used for low-cost furniture) is not confused with "restoration", for which natural glues and special stuccos are normally used - by experts!

Glass-papering

Before commencing the decoration task, the surface must be smoothed off. This applies to both new wood which has not previously been treated and woods with a thin transparent coating arising from polishing.
Clearly, glass-papering must be performed in relation to the extent of the surface finishing.
Glass-papers are available commercially in a variety of grain sizes.
Progressive numbers indicate the grain size: as n. 150 paper is more abrasive than as n. 320 paper. As well as glass-papers, there are silicon papers with a very fine grain (n. 600, 800) used for polishing. Their polishing power is increased if they are wetted with a little water.
For bare wood, use as n. 230-280 glass-paper lightly to eliminate dirt, dust and minor imperfections.
If the surface has already been coated with paint or varnish, clear or

Side: remove the clamps from the bonded and stuccoed parts and then abrade the stucco-work. Only at this point can the first coat of primer be applied (photo below). Far right: materials used to prepare bases: water-based protective agents, primer and fillers.

otherwise, it is a good idea to begin with a coarse grain glass-paper (n. 150) which is highly abrasive and then pass onto a finer grain (n. 250). This will produce a clean and smooth surface.

Base polishing and touching up

Once the wood has been consolidated, the surfaces to be decorated must be prepared to ensure good adherence. First of all, polish and impermeabilize the surface. To do this, apply a coat of sealing primer (available at ironmongers). It should be diluted (4 parts primer, 1 part turpentine); before applying the product, however, remove every trace of dust from the wood. Apply the primer with a 50 mm boar bristle brush; spread it evenly, because it must penetrate into every crevice of the piece of furniture without forming lumps. Excess sealing primer which may form in these small defects can be removed with a smaller brush; do this before it dries. When the sealing primer is completely dry, finish the surface with glass-paper. Drying times depend on ambient humidity and the thickness of the coating; generally this takes about 24 hours but if the room is very humid and the coating rather thick, longer drying time may be needed.

At least two coats are always needed, alternated with glass-papering. For certain decorative effects such as imitation marble, or if the primer has

normal large brush; at least two coats are needed and the wood should be lightly glass-papered between coats. This clear preparation does not create a compact, white surface ready for decoration, so an extra coat of primer is always required.

Earthenware and gypsum

Local markets always have objects in earthenware (lamps, plates, vases, goblets) or gypsum (cornices, medallions), both plain and decorated. If such objects are not already decorated, they can be as personalized as you like, adapting them to every kind of furnishing environment. Earthenware and gypsum are both very porous and friable materials and must therefore be treated before they can be decorated. Earthenware objects should be immersed in water for several hours and left to dry for some time; when they are completely dry, glass-paper them (paper n. 230) and then treat with a

Now that the base has been prepared with primer, the chair (left) is ready to be decorated.

been diluted too much and therefore doesn't completely cover the veins of the wood, the base should be glass-papered lightly (glass-paper n. 220) and treated again with at least three coats.

As well as sealing primer, another opaque priming base is available for wood, which is diluted in water rather than turpentine; it is also available from ironmongers.

In comparison with sealing primer, this product is undoubtedly more practical since it is easier to apply and dries more quickly (less than 24 hours). However, because it provides less coverage, more than three coats are necessary; overall, it gives a less compact and less honed final result.

Throughout the book, explanations will be provided when it is preferable to use this water-based product. If it is necessary to retain the natural colour of wood without covering it completely with water-based paint, or if a white base is not required, use an impregnation product such as grain filler or thyxatrophic filler to fill the pores. It is a transparent liquid, not dense and easily procured; it does not have to be diluted. The filler is applied rapidly with a

water-repellent coating (transparent or white if the base needs to be lightened). If a covering product is selected, it should first be diluted (1:1) and then applied to the surface (inside and outside) with an ox bristle brush, taking care not to leave brush marks. After about 24 hours, if necessary, glass-paper the object again with the same paper. Wait a further 24 hours before beginning the decoration task.

An earthenware vase lightly smoothed off with glass-paper to polish the surface.

Gypsum is already white so further lightening is unnecessary but it is much more porous and friable than earthenware.

Begin with light glass-papering (again using paper n. 230) to smooth off any surface imperfections, then apply a coat of water-based paint (diluted 1:2) over the entire object. It can be decorated a few hours later. For both earthenware and gypsum, it is advisable to use dilute water-based colours so that too thick a film does not form. The decoration does not require any finishing lacquer (except, perhaps, for a thin coating of water-based lacquer) since too thick a film would adhere poorly to the base. To make the object more luminous, it can be treated with a little wax. Bear in mind that these objects should be used with care to avoid scratching the decoration.

Top: to lighten the base colour of the material and prepare the earthenware for decoration, a base coat of lightly diluted water-based primer is applied to the surface. Centre: an earthenware vase decorated with an imitation marble effect. Below: two stages in preparing gypsum. Firstly, glass-paper the surface (left) and then apply a coat of diluted water-based paint (right).

Walls

A bare wall at the end of a corridor, a niche, a room without windows - all these are places where the need for some form of decoration is often felt. The ideal base for a wall decoration should be white, smooth, hard, clean and dry. It must also be compatible with acrylic and water-based paints.

If there are traces of damp on the wall (indicated by browning, mould or swollen plaster), it is best to call in expert advice.

Such marks, in fact, do not only depend on rising damp or water leaks but also on the condensation which accumulates

on the walls of a rather damp room. If the plaster is badly spoilt, swollen or has gaps - unless the wall is remade - it is advisable to forget the idea of decorating it. On the contrary, old plaster in good condition, even if it has several different coats of old paint, can prove to be a good base for wall decorations.

If the wall has been painted with white water-based paint (emulsion), simply wash it down with water and a slightly abrasive degreasing agent. Then leave it to dry for 24 hours.

If the wall has been painted with distemper (recognized by the trace of powder left on the hands if you rub the wall), the entire surface area to be decorated should be carefully sanded

down to eliminate every trace. To smooth the wall off, sand it with a fine glass paper. Having removed the powder with a soft brush or a dry cloth and before decoration, apply an insulation coating (available in paint shops with full instructions for use). Another way to eliminate distemper is to rub the wall several times with a wet cloth, rinsed frequently in fresh water; apply the insulation coating when the wall is dry.

Walls painted with paint diluted with turpentine are more difficult to prepare (lacquered, waxed walls etc.) In this instance, it is advisable to rely on an expert.

Walls may also have holes, small cracks and old nails. Firstly, remove the nails with pliers; then enlarge the smaller cracks with the tip of a screwdriver and a scraper, so that they can be completely filled with stucco.

Plaster which does not adhere perfectly must also be detached from the wall. Treat the exposed parts with a coarse

It is almost impossible to find a completely smooth wall free of holes, cracks, nails and the like.
To prepare the wall for decoration, remove picture-hooks, nails etc. With pliers, enlarge the cracks with the tip of a screwdriver, sand down and remove surface powder with a brush.

Right: stuccoing small cracks and holes is very important in preparing the wall for decoration. Below: the next stage requires careful sanding to smooth off the plaster perfectly.

be stuccoed more than once and, between each application, left to dry and then sanded. When the plaster is uniformly smooth (use a medium grain glass-paper, n. 180-200) and only when perfectly dry, smooth down the surface again with a very fine glass-paper (n. 240). The powder produced will resemble talc - if not, it means the wall was not thoroughly dry. Drying times depend on temperature and humidity in the room.

To facilitate glass-papering, it is advisable to pass a wet rag over the still-moist stucco to remove any excess; only when the stucco is dry should sanding be performed.

If the base surface is not white, two coats of water-based paint are needed: the first should be more dilute than the second and sanding is required between the coats.

The wall does not always have to be perfectly smooth - it depends on the kind of decoration to be made. For example, in grotesque decorations an imperfectly smooth wall and certain small irregularities may even make the decoration seem older than it really is; in stencil work, a coloured base may be useful. A perfectly white and smooth surface, however, is essential if an imitation marble effect is required. In this instance, treat the wall with two or three coats of primer diluted with turpentine and, between one coat and the next, sand down with a fine grain glass-paper. If you don't want to tackle the tasks involved in preparing the base, call in a painter - explaining the final result intended.

glass-paper (n. 150) and use a dry, clean brush to eliminate every trace of dust and powder.

For stuccoing, use multi-purpose stuccos (available from ironmongers), mixed with water, or ready-to-use stucco pastes (which should also be softened with a little water). Dissolve a small amount of stucco in water in a paper bowl until a soft, uniform paste is obtained. Use this paste to fill areas where plaster is missing (cracks, holes, detached bubbles). Make sure the stucco penetrates fully and remove any excess with a small spatula. Generally speaking, these kinds of crack need to

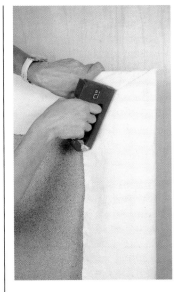

To fix canvas to a rigid frame, begin at the corners and then move down the sides.
The base should be prepared by applying a special paste coating of water and gypsum. Preparation is completed by glass-papering the entire surface to a smooth finish.
A special stapler can be used to secure the canvas to the frame (bottom).

Canvas

Canvas can also be used as a base for interior wall decorations, provided it is prepared for this purpose. Art shops sell canvas which is already prepared for painting with acrylic paints. It is very expensive and, considering the quantity needed for a wall decoration, it is preferable to prepare the base personally.

The best canvas should be untreated in cotton or linen, thick and with a large weave. The canvas should be stretched over a rigid frame (such as MDF), folded over the edges of the frame itself and secured with a stapler (an operation best performed by two people). It should then be impregnated with a special compound prepared by mixing three parts of water and three parts of Bologna gypsum; when the paste liquefies, add a small part of acrylic glue (100% acrylic emulsion) to densify. This paste, which must be stored for some days, should be applied uniformly, "pulling" it evenly with a 1 cm ($1/2$ in) high boar bristle brush (i.e. 70 or 80 mm); the brush should be used initially in a horizontal direction and then, when the canvas is dry (24 hours) vertically. Sand down with n. 230 glass-paper.

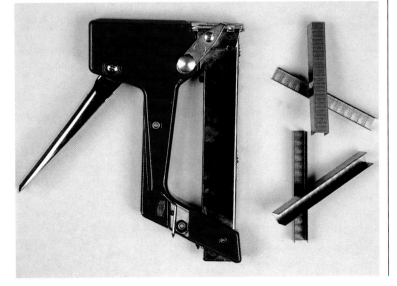

BASE DECORATION

The kind of decoration of the base of a piece of furniture or an object can be chosen in different ways. What really matters is to bear in mind that the base is extremely important for the final result and, especially, must integrate fully with the colour and the style of the object and the decorative elements.
If you are undecided, opt for a uniform base which adapts well to all kinds of decoration and, if accompanied by an antiquating finish, is ideal for Country and Tyrolean décor.
To obtain a uniform base, at least three coats of paint are needed; sand down lightly between each coat (glass-paper n. 230). The paint should be slightly diluted and applied only having first moistened both the brush and the surface; brush on lightly, avoiding obvious brush marks. The paint can even be diluted further to make this task easier.

Sponging technique

There are two kinds of sponging technique: "sponging-off" and "sponging-on". The former is best suited for delicate sponging in which the base colour is revealed. If a transparent basic white colouring is not required, apply the new colour, wait until it dries and then "sponge-off".
Initially, prepare a sufficient quantity of paint (three spoonfuls are enough to cover around 1 sqm/11 sq ft) and dilute with water to produce a rather fluid but nevertheless covering liquid; apply the paint to the moistened surface with a 40-50 mm mane brush. The paint should be applied uniformly without worrying too much about the brush marks, since sponging will hide them. It is preferable to paint small areas, one at a time, since sponging has to be performed before the paint dries. Having applied the colour, take a wet, squeezed sponge and dab the surface, removing paint to produce an orange peel effect, i.e. leaving the base colour just visible. The second technique - "sponging-on" - helps achieve a more or less intense sponging

Right and below: the "sponging-on" technique with a chair prepared with a primer and glass-papering. The final effect itself is highly decorative. Bottom right: the initial stage in the "sponging-off" technique.

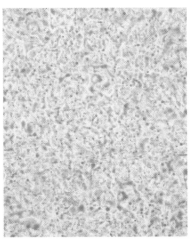

From the left: the second stage in the "sponging-off" technique and the final effect.
Centre and below: the "sponging-on" technique and the final effect.

effect and is more practical than the former technique when decorating large surfaces. As for "sponging-off", the base must be moist and the paint rather diluted. But in this case, the paint is applied with the sponge, dabbing it quickly and uniformly over the surface before it dries. Never apply the sponge again to drying paint to avoid removing it: wait until everything is dry and then fill in empty spaces. If you notice the paint thickening during the "sponging-

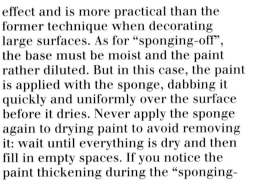

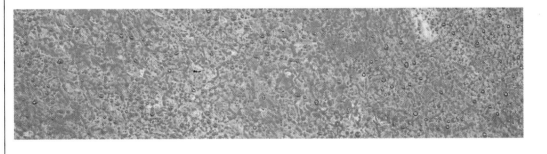

on" process, it means it was not diluted enough; the remedy is to dab more forcefully.

HINTS AND TIPS

For a good sponging effect, it is advisable to use a very jagged natural sponge, which must always be clean. Do not rotate the sponge but hold it firmly in the hand and dab with constant vertical movements. In "sponging-off", begin along the edges of the coat of paint just applied so that it doesn't dry and form halos; then move inwards. If the surface is drying, add a little more fresh paint (more dilute) over the top; this will give more time for the sponging operation. The paint to be sponged must be rather moist, otherwise there is the risk of spotting the surface instead of achieving an orange peel effect.

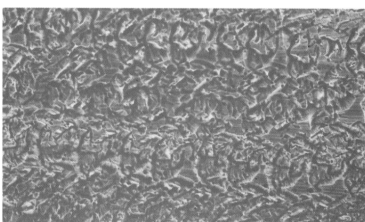

From the top: stages and final result of sponging with a rag and paper. Right: an example of wood (Douglas fir) treated with the distemper pickling technique.

Sponging with a rag and newspaper

This technique resembles sponging, not least in the way it is performed, however it does not produce an orange peel effect. In place of the sponge, use a newspaper or cloth which should be well crumpled; the folds then reproduce a sponge-like effect. Many rags or balls of newspaper should be prepared beforehand, since they cannot be rinsed and re-used when saturated with paint, otherwise they lose their folds; obviously, they cannot be washed like sponges. Before starting this task, it is a good idea to practise with a wooden panel, bearing in mind that the effect on this sample will differ from that obtained over a larger surface.

Pickling

In the past, fir and pine used to build houses (especially in America) were disinfected with caustic soda - which penetrated into the fibres of the wood, whitening it and highlighting the vein structure. In the early 20th century, this type of effect also became popular in Europe, especially in France, and wood was treated in this manner not so much for practical as aesthetic purposes.
If you have an object in soft wood with good veining which is worth emphasizing, specific products can be

Mottling effects.
Far left: surface treated with a uniform coat of water-based oxide red paint.
Left: once the paint is dry, a thick layer of lime putty is applied, which is then marked with a scraper (below).
Bottom left: detail of the effect obtained and, right, the finished object.

used (available in large DIY centres) or distemper, available from ironmongers. The technique is very simple.

Apply a generous coating of not very fluid distemper (dilute with water) to the bare wood; brush on well and leave to dry. When the base has turned pure white, wipe over with a moist sponge and wait until the surface dries again, highlighting the veins. Lastly, apply a coat of water-based protection compound.

This base decoration technique used to highlight wood is ideal for Country décor and can be enhanced with other simple decorations applied on top of the protective coating.

A pleasing mottled effect can be achieved if lime putty is used instead of distemper (not to be confused with caustic lime, which is very dangerous). Before applying the lime putty (which can be diluted in water), apply a coat of slightly diluted water-based paint: choose strong colours contrasting with white. When the lime putty has turned white and powdery to the touch, it can be scraped off in the same direction as the veins.

This technique is best suited to simple, modern furniture, since the effect obtained is very pleasing and requires no further decoration.

Using mordant dyes

If you own fine furniture or objects in highly prized wood, with excellent veining, which do not need stuccoing or repairing, then it is preferable not to cover the surface with superfluous

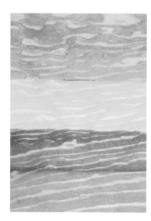

Above: a lampshade base treated with cherry and ebony mordants.
Top: a water-based mordant is applied with a brush to a panel of bare wood: note the difference in the base colour.
Centre: samples of coloured aniline.

decorations. In this case, mordant dyes can be used to enhance the colour of the wood without covering it.

This technique is often used in rustic decoration.

Various kinds of mordant are available commercially; they are usually aniline in the form of powders diluted in alcohol or water.

There are also ready-to-use products, generally oil-based, in the form of liquids, gels or creams; in this case, simply follow the enclosed instructions and observe closely the colour shades which can be achieved. Oil-based products dry quite slowly and this means they can be applied more easily. If using anilines diluted in water or alcohol, it is advisable to try out different dilution strengths on a sample.

Anilines are available in various colours (brown, blue, red, vermilion, lemon yellow or black) which can also be mixed to obtain different shades.

There are also water-based mordants which may require several coats alternated with light glass papering (paper n. 230), since the water tends to raise the fibres of the wood.

Mordants which are diluted in alcohol, since they dry quickly, may leave the colour darker when passed over with the brush.

Whatever kind of mordant is used, it is a good idea to try it out on a sample of wood first (or a hidden part of the object), since all woods react in different ways depending on their type and the final colour may turn out differently to what you were expecting. If, when using an oil-based mordant diluted in turpentine, the colour is not uniform because of errors in brushing on or dosing the product, the remedy is to wipe the most coloured part immediately with solvent.

To apply ready-to-use cream or liquid products, use a cotton or wool rag (taking care not to leave fibres on the surface) or two brushes of different sizes: one for larger surfaces and the other for milled surfaces.

If anilines are to be used, dissolve the mordant powder well in water or alcohol, dip the brush in the product

to repeat the same colour shade should the original mixture not be enough to complete the task.

The amount of alcohol used determines the volume and the shade: if the colour needs lightening, add more alcohol. The liquid should then be applied with a brush, rapidly and "pulling" well. When the surface is completely dry it must be coated with a bituminous fine arts

and apply rapidly to the surface. Avoid applying over areas already treated as this can intensify the colour in an irregular manner. Only when the product is dry can a second coat be applied to intensify the colour. At the end of this task and before starting the decoration, apply a coat of filler and a coat of water-based protective compound. The latter, which does not let the paint penetrate into the wood, allows the project to be completed with further decorative elements.

Coloured anilines can be used to achieve a special decorative effect: new wood can be made to look "old".

To give the base the appearance of "aged wood", mix very little yellow and red aniline powder with alcohol. The resulting liquid is clear orange; prepare a generous amount, since it is difficult

varnish, mixed with oil or essence of turpentine and applied with a rag or a brush. Wait until the varnish dries and then sand delicately with glass-paper n. 220.

Finish with wax to accentuate the effect of old wood.

Left: a ready-to-use cream mordant applied with a soft cloth.
Below: preparation sequence for producing an "aged wood" effect. The wood is dyed first with aniline; a coat of bituminous varnish is then applied; lastly, the surface is lightly glass-papered.

A simple wooden seat in ordinary wood can be enhanced using the "scratched varnish" technique to produce an "aged" appearance; stencil decorations repeat the motifs of the cushion.

Top left: the first stage in the "scratched varnish" technique involves a coat of water-based paint. When this is dry, a truncated brush (right) is used to apply a little pure wax and an antiquating product, in certain parts.

"Scratched varnish" technique

The "scratched varnish" technique can be used to give wood an "aged" appearance. The surface will appear as if the top coat is worn, revealing the underlying coats. Even the decoration will appear older than it really is. This technique is ideal for Country décor, but should be used only with reproduction furniture.

Use a 50 mm brush to apply a coat of the colour to be seen through the scratches over the surface.

The paint should not be diluted too much since it must provide good coverage.

When dry, use an 8 mm bristle brush to apply pure wax only in the parts typically subject to most wear and tear, such as the drawers and tops of furniture.

Remove the excess wax and blur the edges with a rag.

The final colour should be applied with a brush to cover the first coat completely; if contrasting colours are used, the effect will be even more

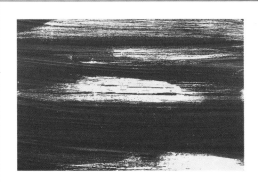

HINTS AND TIPS

If mistakes are made during the "scratched varnish" technique, they can be remedied by applying a coat of very dilute antiquating product. The white of the base will become beige and will seem older. The other *colours will yellow slightly in harmony with the final "ageing" effect (top). Excess wax gives a peeled rather than a scratched effect (right).*

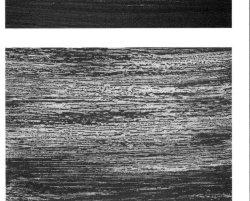

apparent. If the colour does not adhere very well, this is probably caused by excess wax; wait for a few minutes and repeat the operation.

Wait patiently until the paint dries and then use a rag soaked in turpentine to rub over the surface. The first coat will be revealed where the wax was applied. This movement should not be circular but from left to right, since this will produce blurring, which can be accentuated by light glass papering with paper n. 180; be careful not to remove both coats of paint.

Above, left to right: how excess wax is "pulled" and the second coat of high contrast water-based paint is applied to produce a final uniform coating.
Left: the movement of the cloth soaked in turpentine.

Base decoration techniques

As previously mentioned, it is very important to select the "base decoration" technique in order to achieve a particular kind of pictorial effect. Every decorative style has its specific approach to base preparation. Bear in mind that a decoration is not necessarily a defined figure, such as a flower, a leaf and so on. There are ways of applying colours which in themselves "decorate" the base prepared using the techniques described above.

During the "mottling" process, the brush must be held correctly, as shown in the top photo. If it is held in the wrong way, as shown in the right-hand photograph, the stipples will be irregular and elongated. If the paint is too dilute, the mottles will appear as pale marks (bottom photograph).

Before commencing the final decoration task, it is a good idea to practise on a surface prepared with primer to gain the necessary dexterity and to avoid errors. Once the basic rules have been learnt, it is not difficult to take up any form of decoration.

"Mottling"
This is used especially for imitation marble and on sponged bases to enhance them.
"Mottling" literally means applying spots of colour contrasting with the base. The mottles are produced by flicking a stub brush with the index finger (the bristles are held in place by paper tape applied at the base).
The tip of the brush once prepared is dipped into the paint (without wetting the tape) and any excess should be dabbed onto a paper towel.
The paint used for mottling must be diluted so that it is fluid but not watery; it is essential that it retains its ability to cover the surface.
Holding the brush at right angles to the surface (which must be dry), flick the bristles with the index finger. Move the hand gradually to produce uniform mottling over the entire surface. The brush should be held at a distance of about 10 cm (4 in).
When working on a large surface, the size of the brush and the distance away from the surface must both be increased.
A toothbrush can be used to produce very tiny, uniform dots.

HINTS AND TIPS

When mottling, the consistency of the colour is very important. If the paint is diluted too much, the stipples will be almost invisible when dry; on the contrary, if the paint is too thick, mottling will be very difficult.
It is a good idea to try out *the effect beforehand on a newspaper, so that the intensity of the colour can be adjusted. Move the brush vertically over the surface, so that drops of paint fall away; if any drops do fall on the surface, wipe them off immediately with a paper towel.*

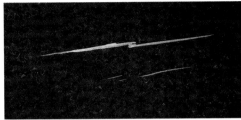

Left: a Marquina Black marble effect with straight veins (the easiest to draw). The brush should be held as shown in the photo.

Veining

It is extremely important to learn the veining technique, not only for imitation marble effects, but also as a way of practising brushing skills.

There are various kinds of vein; straight, small and wavy, fine and criss-crossed, classic and cloudy.

Always ensure that the surface where veining is to be applied is moistened. Dip the tip of a synthetic sable retouching brush into the diluted paint (the size of the brush should be appropriate to the area to be decorated) and proceed with a firm hand.

Veining should always "fade away" and never come to a clear-cut end. Small,

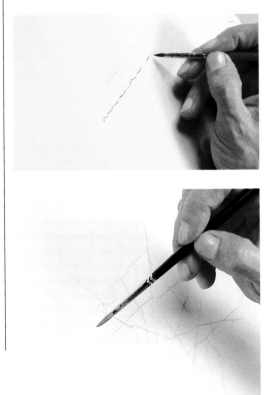

wavy veins are made using a 2 mm synthetic sable retouching brush and a well-diluted colour. The line should tremble but nonetheless move in a straight direction.

For fine, criss-crossed veins, use a very thin retouching brush (about 3 mm) and an even more diluted colour (it must appear almost like a shadow); the lines of the veins must be continuous and of equal thickness and intersect each other to form a highly irregular network.

Classic veins are distinguished by a wavy, and irregular pattern which follows a certain direction; begin with a certain thickness and gradually make

Above: drawing a typical veining pattern.
Top left: small, wavy veins (typical of imitation "lumachella carnica" marble); bottom: the network of veins, which can be smaller or wider depending on the type of marble.

37

To give veining a naturally tremulous appearance, keep your hand off the surface (photograph right). Below: veining typical of imitation Sienna yellow marble.

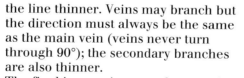

the line thinner. Veins may branch but the direction must always be the same as the main vein (veins never turn through 90°); the secondary branches are also thinner.

The final impression must be one of a mark left by a drop of water running down a windowpane: it trembles and if it breaks off into several branches, the direction remains the same and the droplets get gradually smaller. Observe the veining pattern of true marble to understand the concept better.

Classic veins are made using a retouching and a flat brush. As in other kinds of veining, in which the underlying surface is moistened so that

the paint runs better, the base in this instance must also be well moistened; this also prevents the paint drying too quickly and corrections can be made by blurring the colour with a small sponge or a wet flat brush.

To mark out the veining, the brush must be held lightly between finger and thumb and the forearm should not rest on the surface in order to emphasize the tremulous, wavy effect. The veining pattern should be tortuous and pressure must be gradually reduced so that the vein gradually thins out and finally fades away. To blur the colour, use the edges of a flat-tipped brush.

The white marks sometimes found inside large veins are known as "clouds" (lapis lazuli is a classic example); they also appear alone (as in Aver marble). To copy this effect, wet the tip of the selected brush very well with highly diluted paint and cover the centre of the moistened zone, spreading out slightly towards the edges with the brush: the final colour should be denser in the middle, even if somewhat irregular. The end result (you can use a clean sponge for this) should resemble elongated clouds.

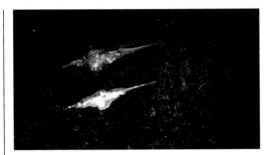

Top left: an example of "clouding" on imitation Marquina black, "serpentina moschinata" and Aver marbles

Bottom left: the same technique used in imitation lapis lazuli to accentuate the depth of the veining.

yellow colouring of wood.
When imitating a marble, it is often essential to veil the surface to distinguish the shade of a colour inside an imitation slab. Here again, the surface should be moistened, the highly diluted paint should be dabbed on in certain areas with a wet sponge. Intensifying this operation on veins achieves a veiling effect which disguises any evident imperfections; moreover, veins seem softer, as if they are set more deeply, and this significantly increases the realism of imitation marble.

Veiling
This term indicates the application of a very dilute colour over an already decorated surface with a brush or a sponge; it is used to change the colour shade, make veining less evident, or to add shading (as in wall decorations such as the grotesque, grisaille or trompe l'oeil).
To change the shade of a decoration totally, again in the case of small surface areas (such as marble inlays, an area of imitation wood in a trompe l'oeil, etc.), the selected colour must be highly diluted and applied uniformly with a flat brush of suitable dimensions. It is advisable to test the colour first to verify its coverage: brushed onto a piece of white paper, it should be transparent. These veilings are used to correct an unsatisfactory result; in fact, veiling with umber or oxide red changes the shade of a marble or softens the excessive

Photographs above and left: some applications of veiling to change the shade of a wood or (below) give depth to the veining in imitation marble.

FINISHING

Once a surface has been decorated it should be protected against light, knocks and scratches with a protective coating. A wide range of such products is available commercially. Choose the most appropriate protective coating in relation to the use of the object or the decoration.

Water-based protective coatings

These are used to protect surfaces which are not exposed to particular wear and tear and are preferable to other products because they tend not to yellow with age.
There are two types of water-based protective coating: matt or shiny. Matt varnish is generally more suitable. These are viscous, milky and very elastic liquids which become completely transparent when dry. They should be diluted with water (3 parts of product, 1 part water) and applied only once the surface has been cleaned with a moist cloth to eliminate any trace of dust or grease (such as fingerprints).

Use an ox or synthetic bristle brush for acrylic paints to apply the product. The liquid should be "pulled" well to avoid forming droplets; to check whether the coating has thickened or is missing in certain parts, observe the surface against the light. If there are gaps, dip the brush again in the product and apply over these gaps. If there are small droplets, clean the brush with newspaper or a rag and "pull" the droplets to eliminate them. When the first coat is completely dry (generally after a few hours), at least one more coat is needed.
Glass-paper the lacquered surface delicately between coats, with a circular movement using moist n. 600 silicon paper (pass the paper rapidly under running water).
Remove any residual traces of dust with a moist cloth and, if preferred, wax and antiquate.

Right: a chest decorated by hand with rustic motifs is treated with a coat of wated-based protective agent.
For right: an imitation marble top is protected with a shiny oil-based lacquer.

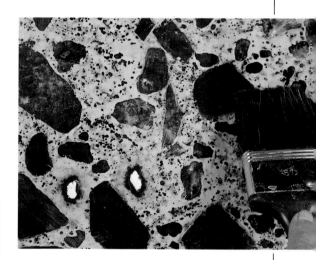

Oil-based lacquers

In comparison with water-based products, oil-based lacquers, which can be diluted with turpentine, are more viscous and are thus more difficult to apply and dry more slowly. On the other hand, they ensure better protection and are recommended for protecting surfaces which are subject to

considerable rubbing. Shiny and matt-finish oil-based lacquers are available commercially. At times, depending on the brand, these two versions can be mixed to achieve a medium finish similar to that obtained with wax.
If this solution is chosen, mix two equal parts of the two products and then mix them 2:1 with turpentine. This will take some time; if lumps form, filter the liquid through a fine sieve (like a sieve used for icing sugar - but remember that the sieve can't be used for sugar again! Or a pair of ladies' tights). If the lacquer is solid (but not dry), warm it in a water bath to liquefy.
Then clean the surface to be lacquered with a dry cloth and only then apply the product, delicately and rapidly using a clean, dry 50 mm ox bristle brush. Begin application from the centre so that any concentrations can be spread outwards. Be careful never to pass over an area which is already drying, since there is the risk of leaving brush marks on the surface. Before the lacquer dries completely, try lightly to spread out any concentrations which may have formed with a brush dipped in turpentine.
Wait until the lacquer is dry (at least 24 hours) and then apply the next coat. Rub the surface lightly with circular movements using a moist n. 600 glass-paper, as for water-based protective coatings, between coats. If a shiny lacquer is used, it is best not to glass-paper the top coat, since it would become less bright. Oil-based lacquers tend to yellow with age but just two coats provide a protective film much thicker than that attainable with water-based products.

Polyurethane gels

These gels do not require dilution and are more transparent than oil-based lacquers; they are easier to apply and are available in shiny and matt-finish versions.
The shiny version gives a glass-like finish, while the appearance of the matt version is more natural.
It is preferable to use these gels for small objects and only if they do not have to be antiquated or waxed.
The gel is applied with a perfectly clean and dry 50 mm ox bristle brush. Dip the brush directly into the can and apply it to the surface: try not to create lines. A second coat is needed 24 hours later. Glass-papering is not required.

Above: a polyurethane gel is applied to an object prepared with a cherry-coloured mordant.
To be sure of the final result, it is advisable to practise at first on a sample panel treated with the same base coating.
Bottom: wax is applied with a brush.

Wax

Having lacquered a surface with a water- or oil-based product, it can be waxed to achieve a more natural appearance. Wax is applied with a brush; wait for about one hour and then polish with a clean cloth that doesn't lose fibres (an old woollen vest is ideal).

Antiquating

Antiquating enhances decorations on wood by making them appear older than they really are.

A variety of products are available commercially for this purpose and include liquids or creams which promote a more "seasoned" appearance. Some of these, if diluted with

turpentine, create a less intense effect. The product should be applied to the entire surface with a 30 or 40 mm bristle brush; before it dries, rub it with a soft cloth to make the patina less uniform. Don't forget that the effect will be even more natural if a greater amount of product is worked into the crevices of the item, where it is more likely that time has left its marks.

The final effect is that of an old piece of decorated furniture. Dust down with a clean, dry cloth.

A good antiquating effect can be achieved by preparing the patina with a bituminous varnish (available from ironmongers). Bear in mind that the antiquating patina makes the colours much less bright; before using it, it is therefore best to have a trial run in a corner of the wood to verify its effect on the decoration. Take a glass jar with a stopper and dissolve the tip of a teaspoon of bituminous varnish in three fingers of turpentine and then add three spoonfuls of drying agent plus one of baked linseed oil (both available from ironmongers). Mix with a wooden stirrer and wait 24 hours before using the product. During this time, leave the jar open so that any excess turpentine evaporates. Having completed the procedure, close the jar properly, since the bituminous varnish can be stored for several months if kept well; if, when using the product again, it has dried, add a little more turpentine and drying agent. This liquid should be applied to the surface prepared with one or more coats of water-based protective compound: use an old brush reserved exclusively for this purpose. Before it dries, wipe with a cotton cloth or paper towel to "pull" it better and remove any excess. The effect differs in relation to the amount removed. It is a good idea to leave more in the grooves and, if the effect of accumulated dirt is to be accentuated, add a little talc and treat again some time later with a clean, dry brush. When the surface is completely dry (usually after 24 hours depending on the amount of drying agent used) and is not tacky to the touch, wipe with a moist cloth to remove the excess. Finish with a coat of wax.

Above: a top decorated
with imitation marble
inlays and aged with an
antiquating patina.

Above: a polished and
waxed rustic furniture
item.
Right: a photograph
frame with inlays of
imitation wood treated
with a water-based
protective compound.

ORNAMENTAL DECORATION

Design and colour are decisive factors in every kind of decoration, since they determine harmonious inclusion in the surrounding environment. For this reason, it is advisable to study the other elements in the room thoroughly before beginning the decoration task. When selecting a decorative subject, inspiration can be taken from the design of fabrics or wallpaper in the room where the new decoration is to be made, or from books about furnishing or botany. Other excellent sources are magazines and specific publications which provide a large number of decorative designs, depending on the style or period. This doesn't mean copying; artists in every age have studied and exploited works already completed by others.

Whatever the starting point, once the decorative motif has been chosen it has to be adapted to the surface to be decorated. Once the subject has been enlarged or reduced, it has to be transferred. To do this, it is best to use graphite paper (available from art shops) rather than carbon paper, since the latter may irreparably spoil the base surface. Before using it, graphite paper should be rubbed with a paper cloth to remove excess powder, which might otherwise mark the surface. Having chosen the exact point at which the decoration is to be made, as well as its layout, attach the design, using paper tape, on one side only, so that the graphite paper can be inserted between it and the surface. This insert can then be secured with paper tape with the black face downwards.

Having prepared the surface, the design must then be traced out with a coloured pen; this gradually highlights the work already performed, avoiding the risk of doing things twice. Be careful not to rub your arm over the design and check every now and then that it has not moved from its original position.

Opposite: inspiration for decorative motifs can be gleaned from books and furnishing magazines. Above: floral motifs used to decorate a table in imitation marble.

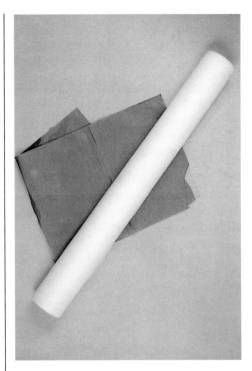

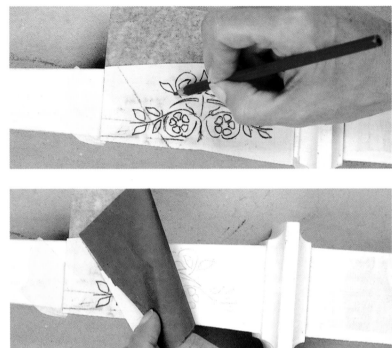

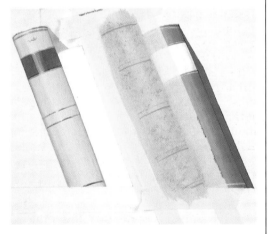

Above: sheets of graphite paper and copy paper.
Right, from top: sequence for transferring the selected design onto an object using graphite paper, in this case a wooden obelisk.
Centre: an example of how to mask the spines of books forming part of a trompe l'oeil effect depicting a bookshelf.
Bottom: a design taken from a book transferred to acetate and transformed into a stencil.

Having completed the transfer operation, pass a moist sponge over the design to remove excess graphite.
In the event of a mistake, do not use a rubber to erase it but first rub energetically with a wet cloth and then glass-paper lightly.

Masking

For Tyrolean and Country decorations, the design can be painted as soon as it has been reproduced, unlike wood or inlay marble effects for which masking is required, since each element in the

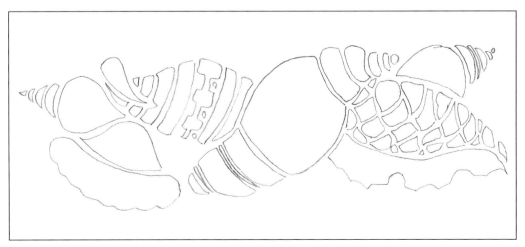

Left: graphite paper is used to transfer the inlay design, which is then masked, onto a wooden surface intended to become a "marble effect" table.
Below: the various stages in producing inlay marble effects.

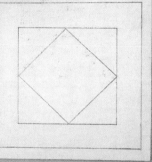

design is painted with different techniques. Masking is also occasionally necessary for wall paintings. This operation is essential whenever there is the risk that surrounding elements already completed may be spoilt by subsequent decoration work. Masking is performed using paper tape which should first be wiped with a cloth to make it less adhesive, thereby avoiding the risk that removal may ruin the base. The tape should be applied and detached using a cutter (without pressing too hard to avoid scratching the surface) so that it perfectly follows the underlying design; the design appears through the tape so that it can be cut out. Firstly, cover the elements of the design which will be painted at a later stage. Having decorated the exposed parts, remove the tape and, slowly and gradually, eliminate any colours which have spread before they dry with a moist cloth. As soon as the painting is dry, position the tape (prepared as described above) over the areas already painted so that those still to be decorated are left free.

To mask small areas (such as small spotting in marble effects), masking liquid for acrylic colours can be used, available from art shops. Brush on

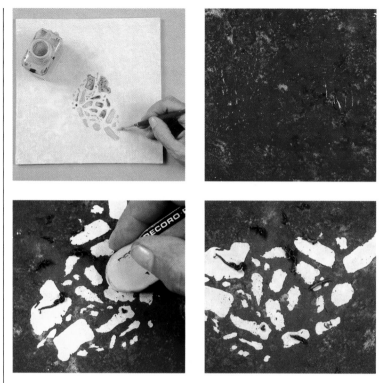

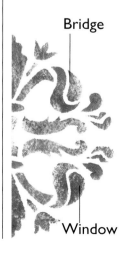

Top: this sequence of photographs illustrates the various stages in masking to produce, using a liquid, the small spotting typical of marble effects.
Below: indication of a bridge and window in a dabbed stencil.
Right: the mask used for a stencil. Notice the vertical and horizontal lines and the repeated design so that the stencil itself can be positioned correctly every time it is used.

Bridge

Window

(remember to clean the brush immediately after use with warm water and soap) over the areas to be protected; when the liquid is dry, the design can be coloured without worrying about affecting the parts protected by this liquid. The protective film is removed with a pencil eraser.

Masks

These are thin sheets of waterproof paper (once in copper, now in acetate or plastic) with cut-outs following a precise design used in stencil-work.
The masks are dabbed with a brush which transfers the colour through the cut-outs onto the base which is to be decorated.
The coloured areas correspond to the holes or "windows", while the uncoloured parts are covered by "bridges".
A wide variety of masks is available commercially but a good decorator ought to be able to produce personalized masks. As well as acetate and plastic, stiff card or parchment can also be used. The latter have to be waterproofed with specific products. Although less resistant, transparent materials make it

easier to trace out the design and dab on the colours, since it is possible to see what is underneath. After use, acetate masks should be cleaned with a moist cloth; if they are not cleaned immediately and the colour dries, then alcohol will have to be used. Be careful not to break them. For jobs involving large surface areas and repeated designs (such as the cornice of a room), it is advisable to prepare more than one mask. Trace the selected design onto copy paper (remember that it can be enlarged or reduced directly onto the acetate with a photocopier) and mark off the borders with a pencil. Then prepare the "bridges", i.e. the strips joining the various parts of the mask which is then cut out to make the "windows". The acetate is then placed on copy paper and an indelible felt-tip pen is used to mark out the design formed by the "windows" and "bridges". To cut out the stencil, place the acetate on a wooden surface and use a very sharp cutter; if a circle has to be cut, don't move the cutter but rotate the mask itself. If the design is rather repetitive (such as a border), prepare a mask which includes not only the cut-out motif but also the start and finish markers, so that when it is positioned on the wall the same distance between one application and another is always

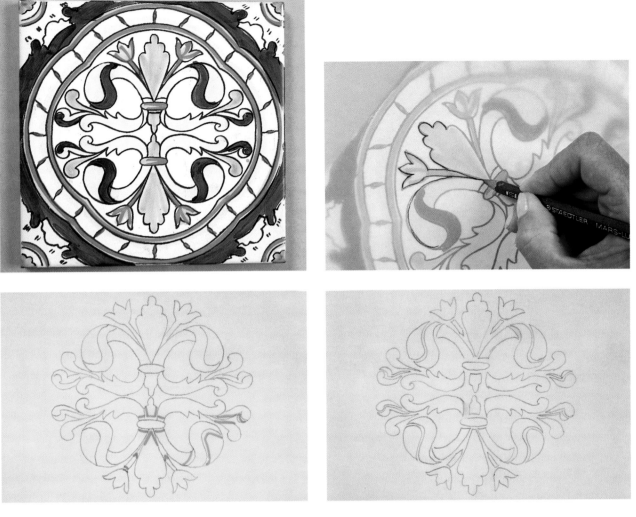

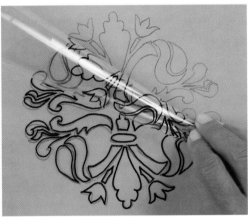

Top: the design of a simple tile transformed into a stencil.
Centre: having copied the design, the "bridges" and "windows" are then marked out.
Bottom: trace out the design on the acetate and then cut out the "windows".

maintained. Always mark the stencil with horizontal and vertical lines: this will make the paint-dabbing operation easier in alignment with vertical and horizontal positions.
Should the mask tear, it can be repaired using a strip of paper tape applied on both sides.

When selecting a decorative motif, bear in mind the object onto which it is to be transferred. Side: the caravel of the voyage of Christopher Columbus on a wooden egg.
Right: how to dip a brush into paint and then remove the excess by twisting it.
Below: two errors in selecting brush sizes: left, the tip is too small in relation to the surface to be painted and the result is "spotted"; right, if the tip is too large, there is the risk of spreading paint outside the design.

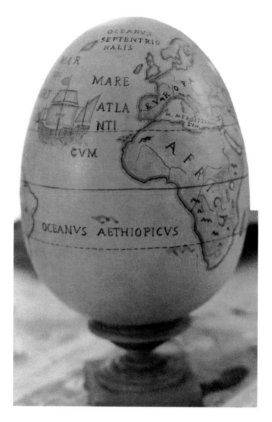

DECOR

In every age, mankind has felt the need to decorate his living environment. Decorative elements clearly reflect the time and place in which they were made. We shall only discuss European decorations, leaving aside those of Africa, South America and the East. By "decorative element", we mean the combination of drawings, scrolls and cornices which embellish an object or a wall. The type of technique and the design itself therefore identify the style of a decoration.

First and foremost, some remarks are appropriate about brush work: brushes should never be saturated with paint and having dipped them into the colour they should be twisted to eliminate any excess.

To make straight lines or borders, rest the elbow and hold the brush vertically in relation to the surface to be painted; try to maintain constant pressure and always brush in the same direction, so that a uniform result is achieved. It is important to keep within the edges of the design, without spreading beyond them; to avoid mistakes, always select a brush of suitable size.

The most common decorative effects are cornices, flowers and leaves; they are distinguished by period and decorative style through their design and the pictorial technique used. Colouring may be flat and plain or shaded. Shading gives decorations relief and roundness; grisaille, on the other hand, even makes it possible to achieve

Examples of decorative motifs of different periods.
1 - Ancient Rome and Classical Greece;
2 - Romanesque, 1400;
3 - Middle Ages, northern Europe (Gothic);
4 - France and England, 16th century;
5 - France, 17th and 18th centuries;
6 - France, 17th century;
7 - end 1800s;
8 - early 1900s;
9 - typical Tyrolean decoration, unchanged from time immemorial.

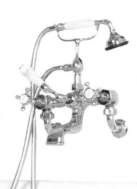

Above: different base colourings highlight the design.
Below: an old cast-iron bath decorated with the same motif used in the flooring; left: detail of the decoration.

three-dimensional effects with light and shade.

To produce shading, prepare the colour in three different luminosities: light, medium and dark. The term "light" used for colours indicates a lighter shade of the base colour, i.e. the medium colour, whereas "shade" indicates a darker effect.

A synthetic sable brush should be used for plain colouring, using a smaller size for darker and lighter shades.

It is essential to use different shades when colouring the various parts of a flower.

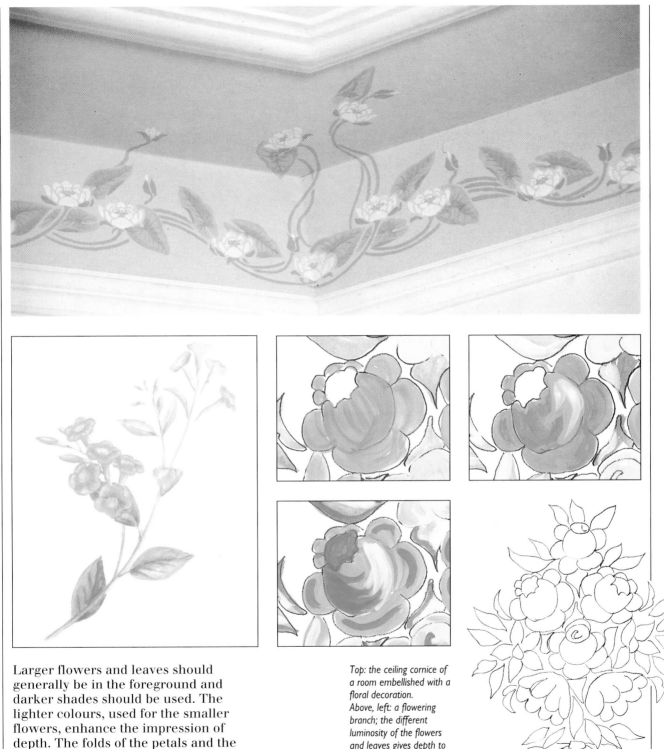

Larger flowers and leaves should generally be in the foreground and darker shades should be used. The lighter colours, used for the smaller flowers, enhance the impression of depth. The folds of the petals and the underside of leaves should ensure contrast to highlight their curvature and shaping.

Colours should be more or less diluted depending on whether coverage or transparent effects are required. It is

Top: the ceiling cornice of a room embellished with a floral decoration.
Above, left: a flowering branch; the different luminosity of the flowers and leaves gives depth to the design.
Above (drawing, right): stages in colouring a bunch of flowers.

HINTS AND TIPS

Borders are formed using straight but not very thick lines (5 mm/ ¹/₄ in), forming a box around a decoration. A steady hand is needed to paint borders; alternatively, paper tape can be adhered to the sides around the space where the line is to be drawn. Now, since there is no risk of spreading outside the area to be marked off, the paint can be brushed on (not too diluted). Remove the tape and repeat the process on another side.

Above: a cornice recalling a classic Tyrolean motif.
Top right: a rose painted with light and shade in all parts.
Above right: different kinds of borders and, bottom, applying paint to a surface protected with paper tape.

54

Left: demonstration of how to rotate the bush when painting Tyrolean décor; this helps achieve the typical light and shade effect.
Below: examples of decorative motifs of flowers and leaves achieved with the same technique.

best to begin with single petals and then, once the paint is dry, identify which areas should be shaded and retouch them with a darker shade (usually the part nearest to the centre of the flower). Then apply lighter highlights in a few places.
To make this operation easier, moisten the surface before applying light and shade effects.
In Tyrolean décor, light and shade effects are produced in a single stroke: the brush is dipped in the paint and the excess is removed; then it is dipped in white paint on one side only. The colours are then applied by twisting the brush, so that the two fresh colours tend to amalgamate with each other.

IMITATION MARBLE

In Rome in the 1500s, renewed enthusiasm for antiquity and studies of archaeological finds encouraged widespread interest in marble and natural stone - the materials used to build Imperial Rome. The multi-coloured marbles of antiquity began to reappear in churches and the palaces of the nobility. It was precisely at this time that marble inlay work became popular. At much the same time, even in northern Europe, wood came to be decorated to imitate marble; in Italy, for example, the balustrades in many provincial churches were decorated in this way. Although this technique emerged as an economic substitute for real marble, it spread rapidly and soon became a form of decoration in its own right.

Before attempting marble-effect decorations, it is a good idea to study the kind of marble you intend to imitate, since every shade of colour must be understood and, in the case of highly veined marbles, the natural flow of the veins themselves (generally rather uniform in most marbles). It is very important to interpret the most characteristic features which, if executed expertly, recreate the effect of real marble. One can begin by copying the veining of a real slab of marble and transferring its appearance onto the surface to be decorated. If a marble inlay is to be imitated, it is essential to reproduce the patterns and colour matches extremely well, rather than simply imitating correctly individual sections of marble which, because they are so small, are not particularly difficult to copy. Study real examples of marble by reading catalogues or books and magazines dealing with antiques.

An attempt to imitate antique marbles, which can no longer be quarried and are known through the works of antiquity, is more rewarding than copying modern commercial materials. The latter, however, are undoubtedly more suitable for beginners, since they are easier to imitate. Imitation marbles are also used in trompe l'oeil, because they enhance the overall subject.

Opposite: a wooden surface imitating marble inlay work; above: the central part of a table in malachite bordered with Sienna yellow and lapis lazuli.

Generally speaking, imitation marble effects are best achieved on a base prepared with sealing primer, although in some cases (which are highlighted throughout the book) good coverage with water-based paint may suffice. The surface must be carefully prepared with glass-paper since it has to be as smooth as real marble. In any case, before deciding what kind of base preparation is needed, it is a good idea to plan the overall project in advance. If an inlay decoration is to be made, prepare the design and then transfer onto the surface to be decorated, masking

Left: a marble inlay of the 1500s. Opposite page, top: a simple vase in imitation porphyry has become a splendid ornament.
Bottom: wooden spheres decorated to imitate ancient marble; from left: multi-coloured Capitoline "breccia"; lapis lazuli; Sienna yellow; antique yellow "breccia".

WHAT'S NEEDED

Bucket, paper plates and cups, sponge, acrylic and water-colour paints, boar and ox bristle brushes, paper towels, stub brush, retouching brushes in synthetic sables of various sizes, toothbrush

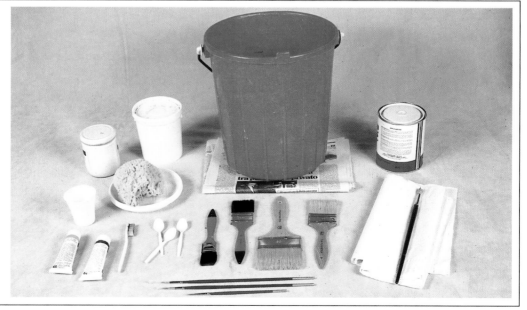

the various parts as necessary. If the design involves a dark base and lighter inlays, transfer it after having prepared the base.

For spherical objects, the decoration must be completed in a single operation, turning the object round in your hands; once dry, any fingerprints can be touched up easily.

With regard to colours, marble materials boast a wide range of shades, so the right shade has to be identified. It is always a good idea to carry out a trial on a sample; for example, colouring a green marble does not always require the use of blue, which is only used if a warm green is used (high percentage of yellow) and subsequently has to be "cooled".

For finishing, should the yellowing typical of turpentine-based lacquers affect the colour shading, apply four or five coats of water-based lacquer, each followed by glass-papering with an n. 800 silicon paper.

To achieve a bright surface finish, apply two coats of pure wax.

"PEPERINO" AND "PIETRA SERENA"

"Peperino" and "Pietra Serena" are both sedimentary rocks and are very similar in appearance. They are widely used, as they have always been, for skirtings, ornamental bands, door and window frames and other decorations.
In the past, "Peperino" was mainly used in many palaces in Rome, while "Pietra Serena" is more frequent in Florence.
These marbles are often reproduced in trompe l'oeil in windowsills, frames, doorsteps or for finishing fireplaces. "Peperino" and "Pietra Serena" may have slightly different shades of colour but are generally very regular; they differ only in terms of the luminosity of colouring and the greater uniformity of "Peperino" compared to "Pietra Serena". As a result, their colours are often very even. The imitation technique is the same for both stones - creating the ideal, waterproof base for wooden table-tops.

1- Slightly dilute dye A or B (use dye A for "Pietra Serena" and B for "Peperino") and, having wetted the surface, begin to sponge it on. Sponging must be uniform so that the colours blend perfectly. This task should be performed for both marbles, changing only the relative colour shade.

2- Then proceed in the same way for dyes C or D respectively for "Pietra Serena" and "Peperino".

3- Dab the dry surface with dye C or D, darkened with a little black.

4- Dab with white when the dark markings are dry. The result can be

Tromp l'oeil imitating a balcony with a window overlooking the countryside with steps and sill in "Pietra Serena".

protected with 2 or 3 coats of clear, water-based lacquer.

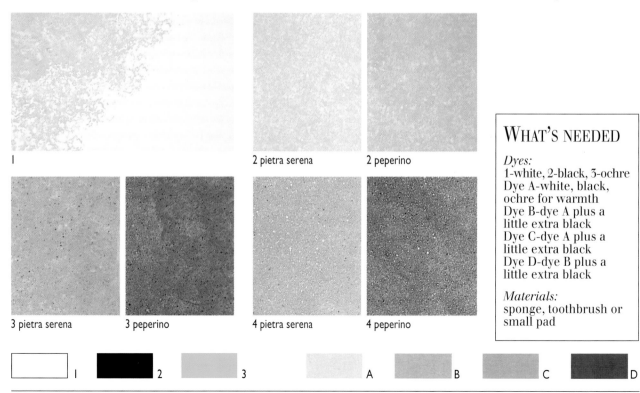

I

2 pietra serena

2 peperino

3 pietra serena

3 peperino

4 pietra serena

4 peperino

WHAT'S NEEDED

Dyes:
1-white, 2-black, 3-ochre
Dye A-white, black, ochre for warmth
Dye B-dye A plus a little extra black
Dye C-dye A plus a little extra black
Dye D-dye B plus a little extra black

Materials:
sponge, toothbrush or small pad

I   2   3   A   B   C   D

RED PORPHYRY

This is a volcanic rock used in Ancient Egypt as a decorative stone. It was used by the Romans for statues and tombs.
This is an easy imitation task ideal for every kind of decoration.
The base is prepared simply with two coats of a water-based sealing agent.

1- Wet the surface and spread dyes A and B (slightly diluted) in distinct areas using two fine brushes. Decide on the extent of these areas in proportion to the dimensions of the surface to be decorated.

2- Before the dyes dry, dab with a moist sponge to achieve an orange-peel effect for both colours, which should finally cover the whole area (the white base should, at most, be barely visible).
Work the sponge over the border areas between the two colours (indicated by the dotted lines in the photograph), so that they blend with each other, alternating the sponge when passing from one colour to the other to avoid transferring the dyes and patting firmly over the two colours.

3- When the surface is completely dry, dab abundantly with black and, when this is also completely dry, with white dyed lightly with red oxide.

1

3

Photograph 2 highlights the borders between the two colours. Below: low relief in stucco-work decorated with a porphyry effect.

The dabs should be of different sizes.
Complete the decoration with three or four coats of clear, water-based lacquer or two coats of clear, thinner-based lacquer.
Wax by hand to achieve natural brightness.

WHAT'S NEEDED

Dyes:
1-red oxide, 2-white, 3-black
Dye A-red oxide plus a little black
Dye B-dye A plus a little more black

Materials:
sponge, small brushes (50 mm), pad n. 8

| | 1 | | 2 | | 3 | | A | | B |

TRAVERTINE

Travertine is a very porous limestone rock. Many Roman ruins were originally built using travertine and over the centuries the stone has been widely used in buildings for windows, cornices and steps, etc. There are several shades ranging from the classic cream colour to nut and red oxide, but the structure of the stone remains very similar. The technique required therefore remains the same even if different shades are used. This kind of decoration, widely used in trompe l'oeil, achieves considerable impact. The ideal base is a water-based primer.

1- Dilute dye A and sponge it uniformly over the moistened surface.

2- Wait until this coat is completely dry, then sponge it with dye B in

A table top decorated with inlay geometrical motifs in imitation marble on a base prepared to resemble Roman travertine.

1

2

3

4

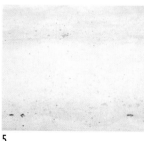

5

WHAT'S NEEDED

Colours:
1-white, 2-black, 3-umber
Colour A-white, ochre to warm, a little umber
Colour B-white plus a touch of colour A
Colour C-umber plus black

Materials:
sponge, 50 mm bristle brush, 6 mm retouching brush in synthetic sable, 8 mm stub brush

certain areas, always moistening the surface so that it can amalgamate with the colour underneath. Then apply a little water-colour C (leaving a little aside) so that when rubbed lightly with a cloth it leaves a grey-brown veiling effect.
The intensity of the colour can be reduced only by adding more water, never white, otherwise the veiling effect is lost.

The result of applying colour C should be that of a slab of travertine

marked by areas of darker colouring which form parallel lines across the surface. When the two sponged-on coats are completely dry, moisten the surface along the imaginary lines of darker colour, dip a

bristle brush of appropriate size (50 mm is ideal), remove excess paint with a paper towel and then lightly and with a slightly trembling hand, apply the veiling. Never interrupt the movement of the brush, otherwise an unnatural break in the colour effect will be produced. Before the colour dries, remove any small lumps and thin out certain parts of the line with a clean, moist sponge to achieve a less uniform effect.

3- Dilute the remaining colour C dye slightly and design the larger pores typical of travertine with a retouching brush in synthetic sable. The "spots" should have an irregular shape, with the centre somewhat darker to create the impression of depth.

4- Sketch out irregular and elongated lines along the first ones with a darker colour, then dab lightly with the sponge to deepen the shade.

5- To achieve a good finish, two or three coats of matt water-based lacquer should be applied.

1 2 3 A B C

"LUMACHELLA CARNACINA"

An organogenetic stone which was not particularly widely used in the past. Over and above its unusual colour, it is characterized by marine fossil remains; for this reason, in pictorial decoration the preference is to imitate the effect rather than achieve a faithful reproduction. Since this is an ancient marble, it is ideal for decorating classic objects, such as spheres, obelisks and inlay table tops. For this decoration, it is advisable to prepare a surface in sealing primer finished perfectly with glass-paper, however for small objects, it is possible to use a matt water-based coverage, treated to produce a very smooth surface.

Table top decorated with inlay motifs in imitation marble on a base prepared to resemble "lumachella carnacina" stone.

1- Apply a uniform coat of colour A, having first diluted it, to the base moistened with a sponge; use an ox bristle brush to ensure even coverage without brush marks.

2- When colour A is perfectly dry, sponge colour B (well diluted) onto certain areas; then use the clean side of the sponge to shade and colour and to amalgamate it with the base.

3- Dilute colour B even further and, later when the surface is completely dry, intensify the colouring of the darker areas with a retouching brush in synthetic sable, especially around the edges. Using a 4 mm synthetic sable retouching brush, apply fine, trembling veins of various lengths with diluted umber. Complete the decoration with a veiling effect in certain parts to intensify the surface colour even more. Use a sponge with a very diluted colour. Five or six coats of water-based lacquer will help achieve greater depth; two coats of wax will give the decoration the brightness typical of marble.

I   2   3

WHAT'S NEEDED

Colours:
1-red oxide, 2-umber, 3-white
Colour A-white, a dash of umber and ochre to warm
Colour B-red oxide, umber

Materials:
sponge, 50 mm ox bristle brush, 4 mm retouching brush in synthetic sable

A solid wooden ball decorated with imitation "lumachella carnacina".

I   2   3   A   B

LAPIS LAZULI

Lapis lazuli is a mineral found in aggregates in sodalite.
Thanks to its ultramarine blue colouring with veins of various shades, it is used as a gemstone and for artistic objects. Lapis lazuli decoration is easy to create and highly effective; it is ideal for old objects, such as lamps, or to give added impact to a plain terracotta vase or a simple wooden cornice. The process, which is very easy, requires the base to be prepared well.

Some typical objects decorated with the imitation lapis lazuli effects.

I

2

3

WHAT'S NEEDED

Colours:
1-ultramarine blue,
2-white, 3-black
Colour A-ultramarine blue
Colour B-light grey (white + black)
Colour C-colour B plus black

Materials:
50 mm brush, 8 mm stub brush, 4 and 6 mm synthetic sable brushes, natural sponge, acrylic glue, bright yellow gold metal powder

1- Moisten the surface with a sponge and quickly apply colour A with a brush. The colour should be diluted but nevertheless ensure good coverage.

2- Dab the entire surface with a moist sponge until an orange peel effect is achieved.

3- Before the colour dries squeeze the

sponge firmly between the fingers until it becomes a kind of wad and then eliminate certain areas of colour to create irregular, elongated areas similar to the veining of marble.

4- When the paint is dry, apply colour B (somewhat diluted) with a 6 mm sable brush to the centre of the lighter shaded

areas produced in step 3.

5- Before colour B dries, blend it with the base by dabbing the edges with a moist sponge (turning it round to the cleaner surfaces), as shown in photograph 3.

6- To achieve an effect of depth over the entire surface, sponge dilute colour C over certain

I   2   3   A   B   C

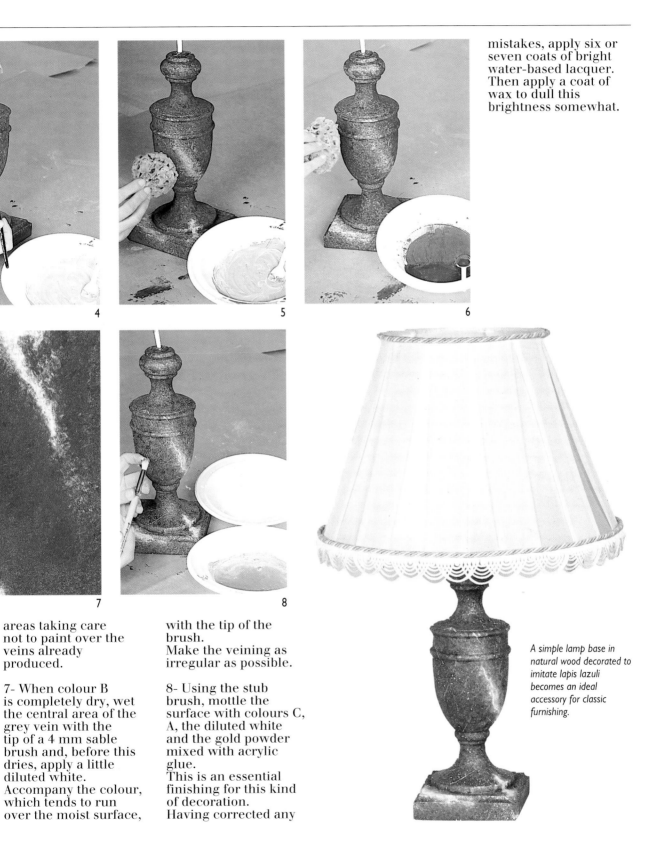

mistakes, apply six or
seven coats of bright
water-based lacquer.
Then apply a coat of
wax to dull this
brightness somewhat.

areas taking care
not to paint over the
veins already
produced.

7- When colour B
is completely dry, wet
the central area of the
grey vein with the
tip of a 4 mm sable
brush and, before this
dries, apply a little
diluted white.
Accompany the colour,
which tends to run
over the moist surface,

with the tip of the
brush.
Make the veining as
irregular as possible.

8- Using the stub
brush, mottle the
surface with colours C,
A, the diluted white
and the gold powder
mixed with acrylic
glue.
This is an essential
finishing for this kind
of decoration.
Having corrected any

*A simple lamp base in
natural wood decorated to
imitate lapis lazuli
becomes an ideal
accessory for classic
furnishing.*

ALABASTER

Highly characteristic thanks to intense veining in various shades of yellow, brown and red, alabaster has been used since ancient times for every kind of luxury object and to embellish cladding. Moreover, the very detailed preparation technique is ideal for inlays.
The shades of colour, depending on various proportions, determine the overall colour of the stone; a variant of flowery alabaster is

WHAT'S NEEDED

Colours:
1-white, 2-ochre, 3-red oxide, 4-black, 5-umber

Flowered alabaster:
Colour A-white, umber, very little ochre to warm
Colour B-colour A plus umber
Colour C-red oxide, black, white
Colour E-ochre
Colour F-white
Golden alabaster:
Colour A for the base
Colour B
Colour D
Colour E
Colour F
Colour G-colour A plus ochre

Materials:
sponge, ox bristle brush, 4 or 6 mm retouching brush

An MDF panel decorated with imitation inlay marble with a central alabaster inset.

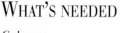

1

2

golden alabaster, characterized by the dominant yellow colouring leaning towards ochre. The colours may vary, but the creation of the two types remains the same. The base must be prepared with sealing primer and be extremely smooth.

1- Apply colour with a brush over the previously moistened surface, brushing in the direction of the

3

| | 1 | | 2 | | 3 | | 4 | | 5 |

veins. To leave as few brush marks as possible, use a rather diluted colour and a soft ox bristle brush. Depending on the final effect to be produced, the base colour can range in shade from cream to light hazel. This means that the shade of the veining will have to be adapted to the base colour. The alabaster in this example was produced using colour A. Wait until the base is completely dry and prepare the various colours needed for the veins on a paper plate. They do not have to be diluted.

2- Take a bristle brush 5 mm ($^1/_4$ in) thick and 10 cm (4 in) wide and then apply the various colours side-by-side with the tip of a retouching brush. Trial and a little experience help match the colours to achieve the desired effect. Nature boasts an infinite variety of colours so it is advisable to put contrasting colours next to each other in different quantities to achieve stripes of different thicknesses.

3- Having lined up these colours on a dry brush, dab it once or twice vertically on a newspaper to help the paint penetrate into the bristles, then brush delicately over the newspaper to remove the excess on the sides. This is essential to avoid applying too much paint and creating veins which are so dense that they remain in relief on the surface.

4- Moisten the surface with a sponge and hold the brush as shown in photograph 3 and apply the paint with a continuous, somewhat trembling, irregular movement with short strokes, slightly increasing the pressure on the surface. In general, it is not possible to achieve veining of equal colour intensity longer than 20 cm (8 in); for this reason, it is a good idea to decorate small areas with this technique. If the required effect is not obtained, immediately remove the colours with a sponge, clean the brush, dry it and repeat the operation changing the colour matching. If the surface to be decorated is wider than the brush, repeat the process on the adjacent section turning the brush round to achieve a mirror effect and repeating the same veining movement.

5- Minor retouching can be performed when the colours are completely dry. For example, a thin line can be added between two veins using a 4 or 6 mm brush and a rather diluted contrasting colour, following the existing outline. In florid alabaster, there are certain small irregularities along some veins which are easy to recreate: simply apply small drops of the same, very diluted colour with the tip of a brush along the veins. Always moisten the surface so that the colour achieves a natural effect by "sliding" over the base.

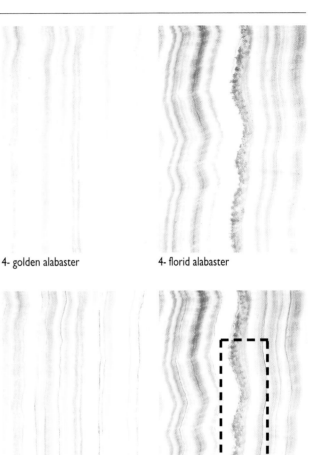

4- golden alabaster   4- florid alabaster

5- golden alabaster   5- florid alabaster

Many coats of water-based finisher give the decoration the depth of marble without affecting the colour shade. Lastly, one or two coats of wax will produce natural brightness.

A   B   C   D   E   F   G

ST. DENIS GREEN

This is a classic marble with intense and very dense veining, used today as it has always been for important, high-impact decorations.
The ideal base for this kind of decoration is wood prepared with sealing primer; it can be performed on small objects and large surfaces thanks to its considerable decorative effect.

1- Dilute colour A considerably and sponge it onto the moistened surface very irregularly.

2- When this coat is completely dry, repeat the operation with colour B (also diluted) passing the sponge over the surface without attempting to achieve an excessive orange peel effect. Leave some areas blank so that the green does not obscure the umber already applied.

3- Having moistened the surface, quickly apply colour C (it must be diluted to avoid forming too dense a coating) with crossways brush strokes, using an ox bristle brush. Moisten the flat brushes; they must have visibly different dimensions. Before the colour dries, pass these brushes over the surface so that the colour is eliminated, creating veins of different sizes in an

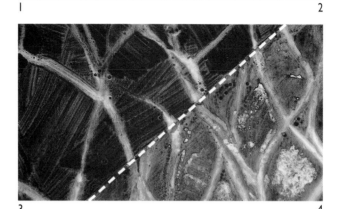

intricate pattern.
You should attempt to create a very irregular criss-cross pattern in which the lines are the veins and the pores the areas painted with colour C.

4- Dab the sponge lightly to make the density of colour more irregular in the areas around the criss-crossing veining.

5- Wait until the surface is dry and apply colour D, again irregularly, so as to intensify the irregularities and the difference in colour shading of both the veining and the base colour.
Use a fine 4 mm retouching brush to design a network of long, tremulous veins in slightly diluted white over the moistened surface. As for all objects decorated with imitation marble effects, especially if they are valuable, finish off with several coats of water-based lacquer and one or two coats of wax.

WHAT'S NEEDED

Colours:
1-white, 2-black, 3-umber, 4-green
Colour A-umber
Colour B-green (ochre as required)
Colour C-green plus black
Colour D-a little black, umber

Materials:
sponge, ox bristle brush, 6 and 10 mm flat bristle brushes, 4 mm retouching brush

Left: wooden obelisk decorated in St. Denis green marble.

	1		2		3		4		A		B		C		D

AVER GREEN

This green marble is less prized than St. Denis but it is still widely used. Thanks to the relatively simple imitation technique, it is often used in trompe l'oeil decorations. It should be mentioned here that when imitating marble on large surfaces, differences in shades should be emphasized. The smaller veins, which embellish decorations of small objects and inlays should give way to larger veins of greater visual impact so that they effectively resemble real marble. This is essential when imitating marble with large table-tops. The base has to be prepared in sealing primer.

1a   1b   2

 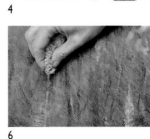

3   4

5   6

7

1- Dilute colours A and B and moisten the base surface. Begin to sponge it to create areas of different colours. The sponge should be rubbed with small, sudden, rotary movements (the faster the movement, the shorter the markings and vice versa) and not dabbed vertically. The required effect is shown in photographs 1a and 1b.

2- To avoid mixing the colours, use two sponges or a single sponge, applying the colours to either side and turning the sponge in your hand as required.

3- When the surface is dry, work over with a moist sponge. To ensure good colour amalgamation, dilute colour C in an irregular manner over the entire surface using the same technique described in step 1 and in the same direction as the underlying paint. The colour should not cover the base layer but leave it visible.

4- Dilute the black quite generously and add a dash of green. Begin applying small straight veins and very elongated "clouds" (moisten the surface in advance).

5 & 6- When the veins are dry, repeat the same operation with white, again using the sponge to shade the colour.

7- If a very large surface area is to be decorated, before adding the veins described apply a few well-spaced larger veins crossing the entire surface. Use colour C (not too dilute) lightened with white.
To achieve greater depth in the various paint coats, it is a good idea to apply many coats of water-based lacquer (at least five). Waxing then makes the brightness of your marble work appear more natural.

WHAT'S NEEDED

Colours:
1-white, 2-black, 3-green
Colour A-white, a little black
Colour B-colour A plus white
Colour C-green, black, very little white

Materials:
sponge, 4 and 8 mm retouching brushes in synthetic sable

The matching of the green colour of this stone with the blue of lapis lazuli is used to achieve the relief effect of a windrose in a table decorated with imitation marble inlay.

1   2   3   A   B   C

"SERPENTINA MOSCHINATA"

This stone dates from Egyptian times. It was called "serpentina" (snake) by the Romans because of its very bright colour and "moschinata" (fly-spotted) because of the dense network of small black intrusions. It is a highly decorative stone and is indicated for both objects and inlay work. It is undoubtedly a very difficult marble to imitate, although the technique is not too time-consuming. However, the final outcome is well worth the effort. The base has to be prepared with sealing primer.

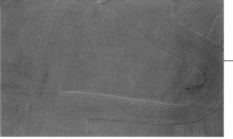

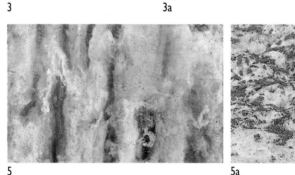

1

2

3

3a

5   5a

1- Having diluted colour A, apply it with irregular brush stokes to a moistened surface. Wait until it is

completely dry and then moisten the surface with a sponge so that the colour runs and achieves a more natural effect.

2- Apply colour B with

a smaller brush, forming irregular whirls through which colour A is visible. Before this coat dries, use the sponge and the retouching brush to make the edges of the

whirls less obvious. Dab the edges delicately with the sponge and move the colour with a very wet brush.

3 & 3a- Wait until the surface dries again and, having moistened it with a sponge, add white using the retouching brush to form clouds of various sizes smudging them with the sponge before they dry (3a).

4- Complete the decoration by covering the entire surface (fully dry) with irregular, tiny black dots.

5 & 5a- Several coats of water-based lacquer and two coats of wax will enhance the natural brightness of the marble once finished (5a).

WHAT'S NEEDED

Colours:
1-blue, 2-green,
3-black, 4-white,
5-ochre
Colour A-blue plus
very little black
Colour B-green plus a
little black and white

Materials:
50 and 30 mm ox
bristle brushes,
sponge, stub brush,
6 mm retouching brush
in synthetic sable

A wooden sphere decorated with "serpentina moschinata".

1	2	3	4	5	A	B

SIENNA YELLOW

A marble quarried in Italy with a compact grain and various shades of yellow, it is highly decorative thanks to its characteristic overall grey, ochre and white veining. Easily and quickly imitated, its warm and delicate colour shades make it ideal for decorating large surfaces.
Since it can be matched with almost all the shades of other marbles, it is also indicated for base decoration of imitation inlays.
It is advisable, given its rapid execution and few coats, to prepare the base with sealing primer.

Lamps, trophies and other small objects decorated in imitation Sienna yellow embellish any setting. Since Sienna yellow is a widely used marble, it is an ideal choice for decorating stucco-work and earthernware.

1- Moisten the surface with the sponge so that the colour runs.

2- Using two brushes, apply colours A and B evenly (well diluted), creating distinct areas in the two shades. Try not to leave brush marks.

3- Before the colour dries, delicately sponge as required to eliminate any brush marks, especially where the two colour shades meet.

4- Sponge colour C onto the surface, without diluting it too much, as soon as the other coats are dry. Before sponging, moisten the surface as always and, with the clean part of the sponge, shade outwards.
Create a well-defined grey area resembling a large vein.

WHAT'S NEEDED

Colours:
1-white, 2-ochre, 3-yellow
Colour A-ochre plus white
Colour B-ochre plus more white
Colour C-white, black, ochre to warm

Materials:
sponge, 50 mm boar bristle brush, 8 mm stub brush, 8 mm retouching brush in synthetic sable, 4 mm flat brush

1

2

3

4

| | 1 | | 2 | | 3 | | A | | B | | C |

5- Depending on the size of the surface to be decorated and the decorative effect desired, other grey areas and veins can be added.

6- Add a dash of black to colour C and use a retouching brush to mark veins in the centre of the grey area just finished.
Wait until the underlying colour is completely dry, so that the surface where these veins are to be added can be moistened.

7- Before this veining dries, shade the colour with a moist flat brush with a trembling movement and irregular jerks.
When the grey veining is completely dry, another vein can be added, using a very dilute ochre colour overlapping the former in certain points to intensify colour.

8- Using absolute white, paint in straight veins crossing the surface at angles to each other. Always ensure that the underlying surface is completely dry before resuming the task.

9- Dilute colour 2 and sponge over the grey veins so as to veil them somewhat. If there are several veins, only some of them can be veiled: this gives the decoration a range of depth.

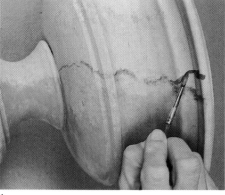

5

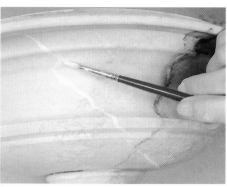

6

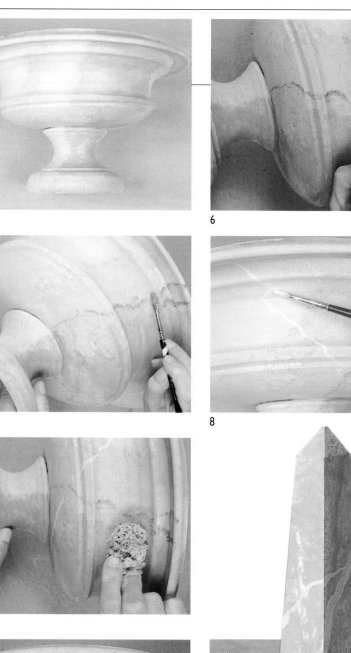

7

8

9

10

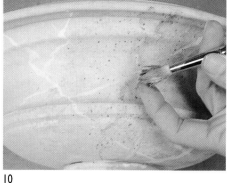

A wooden obelisk decorated to imitate Sienna yellow.

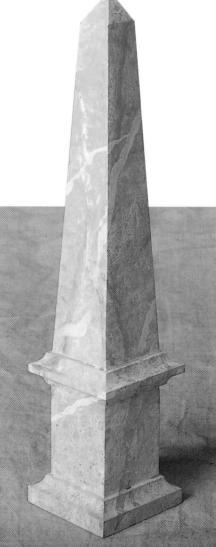

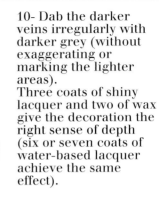

10- Dab the darker veins irregularly with darker grey (without exaggerating or marking the lighter areas).
Three coats of shiny lacquer and two of wax give the decoration the right sense of depth (six or seven coats of water-based lacquer achieve the same effect).

Sienna yellow was selected as the base colour of this large inlay in imitation marble and a small ornament, such as a wooden egg. Below: inlays in Marquina Black on a Sienna yellow base.

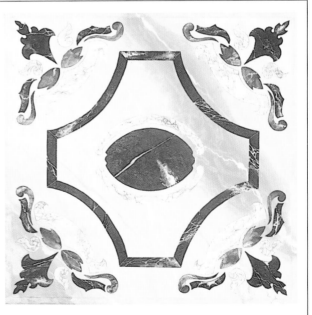

MARQUINA BLACK

Characterized by an intense black colouring with large milk-white veins and small grey veins, Marquina is a highly decorative stone. It is imitated in exactly the same way as Sienna yellow and, since it can be matched with the majority of marble materials (it ensures excellent contrast), it is widely used in imitation marble inlays.
The base can be treated with sealing primer or a coat of water-based white. Dilute colour A and apply it evenly over the moistened surface. Before this dries, sponge delicately; leave the white base visible in certain points. When the surface is dry, paint in the veins with diluted white, using a thin brush for the more irregular and wavy veins. For the straight veins and "clouds", use a stronger white.
This marble must have a highly polished appearance, so, six or seven coats of shiny water-based lacquer or shiny gel (for small objects) should be applied.

WHAT'S NEEDED

Colours:
1-white, 2-black, 3-ochre to warm
Colour A-black plus ochre to warm

	1		2		3			A

ANTIQUE GREEN "BRECCIA"

Greek in origin, this marble has been quarried since Ancient times; it was used by the Romans to produce decorative elements and, given its compactness, even columns. The imitation task for this marble is very long but a water-based preparatory coating suffices.
It is highly decorative but, in view of its complexity, is not recommended for large surface areas.

1- Moisten the surface and then apply colour A (diluted) using irregular brush strokes without worrying about leaving brush marks. Before the colour dries, dab with a sponge in a number of places.

2- Dilute a little white and dilute further with

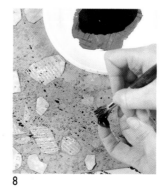

a little green; when the first coat is dry, moisten the surface and create greenish areas and white stripes with a brush.
Also paint in a white spot, which should be surrounded with a halo of dark green.
It is important in this imitation technique that the base be prepared as randomly as possible. The only essential aspect is that the colours should always be diluted and never form dense strata. The decorative effects should be significantly overlapped and intersected to achieve a variety of shades.

3- Cut out pieces of paper to resemble the "breccia" inserts of various types and sizes; they should not be too rounded or too ragged. The majority should be about the size of an old penny.

4- Having prepared the "breccia" pattern, moisten the paper with water, lay them on a cloth and arrange them on the surface. Obviously, if a piece of paper is removed, the underlying surface is revealed; therefore, avoid placing the pattern across two very differently shaded areas; it is difficult to find "breccia" patterning in Nature combining parts in

WHAT'S NEEDED

Colours:
1-white, 2-black, 3-green, 4-ochre (blue)
Colour A-black, ochre to warm
Colour B-green, a little black, white

Materials:
newspapers, scissors, sponge, 50 mm bristle brush, 2 or 6 mm retouching brush in synthetic sable, 8 mm stub brush

| 1 | 2 | 3 | 4 | A | B |

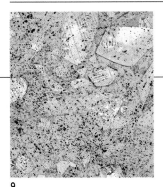

9

10

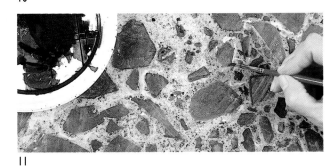

11

12

white, green and black.

5- Position a "breccia" of suitable size on the white spot, so that, once removed, only the white colouring with a green surround is visible, not the black. Arrange the "breccias" at random.

6- Prepare colour B and without diluting it (the water in the paper patterning helps it to run) begin to sponge it over the entire surface; dab delicately to avoid moving the patterns.

7- Do not use much colour. This enables the underlying black to be revealed through the transparent top coat. However do apply denser paint around the edges of the patterns to highlight them.

8- When the colour is completely dry, dot the entire surface irregularly with black.

9- The final effect is shown in the main photograph. Remove the patterns, one at a time, removing any infiltrated colour with a wad of cotton wool.

10- Prepare a little black, a little green and white in a dish. Where necessary, retouch the borders of the patterns with absolute black or black and a little green.

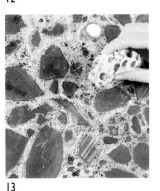

13

14

A lampshade base decorated to resemble antique green "breccia".

11- With the same colours, paint in smaller patterns.

12- Using the retouching brush, moistening it continually with water, produce white veins inside some of the patterns.

13- Moisten small areas of the base with the sponge and create short veils and white veining.

14- The smaller the object, the more likely it will be examined at close range. Therefore the retouching of the base and the patterns must be more detailed. For larger surfaces, in which an inlay effect is achieved, the decoration produced by the structure of the marble itself is sufficient and retouching can be restricted to essential points.
Five or six coats of water-based lacquer will give the necessary depth and ensure that the colour does not yellow with age. Complete with two coats of wax to enhance the natural brightness, of the marble.

MALACHITE

This is a decorative stone of great beauty and enormous value. It is used to produce jewels, precious boxes and, when processed appropriately, to face columns or embellish furniture.
Available in great quantities in the Aural Mountains, it was widely used in Russia to decorate Orthodox Churches and the residences of the Czars. Given the special design technique involved, it is best suited to small surfaces, small objects or inlays. It can also be used to decorate vases and create precious elements in trompe l'oeil decorations. It is essential for this decoration to prepare a good base surface with sealing primer (at least three coats), followed by perfect glass-papering.

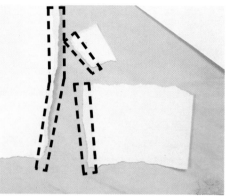

WHAT'S NEEDED

Colours:
1-green, 2-blue, 3-white, 4-black
Colour A-green, blue (only if emerald green is not used), white
Colour B-green (blue), very little black

Materials:
sponge, 50 mm ox bristle brush, card, shiny water-based lacquer

1- Dilute colour A and apply it uniformly to the moist surface; avoid leaving brush marks. Wait until it dries and if required apply another coat of paint, attempting to achieve a very smooth surface.
When the colour is completely dry, apply a coat of shiny lacquer diluted in 1:2 parts water.

2- Prepare pieces of card in various sizes; the best is very stiff, slightly laminated card such as that used in the packaging of cosmetic products or ladies' tights. Tear the card so that edges are as straight as possible; the non-laminated side of the card is used to "pull" the paint.

3- When the surface is completely dry, moisten it with a sponge.

4- Apply colour B in small areas with the larger brush: it doesn't have to be either too dilute or too dense but it is always a good idea to test in a corner to see whether the paint "pulls". If it doesn't leave the underlying surface visible or creates evident lumps, dilute further. If on the other hand it is not possible to recreate the typical stripes of this stone, the paint is too dilute.

5- Hold the card firmly in the hand and place the non-laminated side against the still moist paint. Maintaining the same pressure, "pull" the colour with a continuous movement, zigzagging the hand slightly without creating stripes which are too irregular. This task must be performed rapidly and without hesitation

5

6

7

since it is the only imitation marble decoration, like imitation wood, in which errors cannot be remedied.

6- Before the colour dries, use pieces of card of various sizes to draw the "roses" typical of malachite. Rotate the hand holding the card firmly between the fingers; "pull" the colour with a uniform pressure. Movement should be continuous and not trembling, with jerks, to recreate the characteristic irregularities and avoid producing a circle. This task must also be performed rapidly, before the paint dries - otherwise it will not "pull". Begin with

decorations of small surface areas and only move onto larger areas when sufficient experience and speed of execution have been gained. The paint tends to accumulate in the middle of the design, so it is a good idea to "pull" outwards where the excess can be eliminated with a sponge.

7- Lastly, apply eight coats of shiny water-based lacquer or two or three coats of shiny gel - but only one coat of wax to dampen excessive brightness.

Detail of an inlay table in imitation marble and hard stone such as malachite.

IMITATION WOOD

Just as the technique of imitating marble spread to overcome the scarcity and high cost of marble so imitation wood began to appear towards the middle of the 1600s.

Decorators had significantly refined their experience and problems associated with the supply and increased cost of more highly-prized woods, such as mahogany and palissander, encouraged the use of this kind of decoration. A decidedly Anglo-Saxon taste, the technique was initially limited to transforming less prestigious woods - those with few veins - into more noble materials.

In northern Europe, in particular, skirtings, cornices, doors - especially in service areas or less important rooms - were painted by the decorators of the time to imitate palissander or mahogany. As time passed, the effect became a refined and rather highly regarded art and imitation wood came to be used, like imitation marble, even to embellish the more important rooms in homes. With the onset of the 1700s, this technique went out of fashion, replaced by wallpaper and silk finishing.

Imitation wood thus returned to its role in decorating panels for service rooms. As for imitation marble, before attempting this kind of decoration it is a good idea to gather information about the wood you intend to imitate. As well as studying the flow of veining, it is very important to grasp the shades of colour typical of different woods. Unlike marble, in which the great variety of shades and vein patterns may differ enormously even within a single piece of material, imitation wood decoration must necessarily follow a more restricted approach to realization.

Veining is nothing other than the circular growth lines in the trunk and branches of a tree and its pattern is determined by the cross-section of the cut; as a result, veining patterns are very precise.

Cornices and boxes in MDF or low-cost wood can be given a completely different appearance if they are decorated with inlays of various kinds of imitation wood.

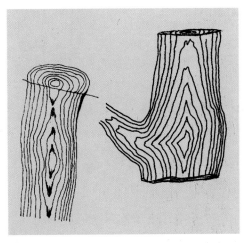

Veining patterns and the broad range of colour shades typical of every wood are the elements which require the most study if effective imitation wood decorations are to be achieved.

As for imitation marble, imitation wood decorations are best started with common wood materials, because they are easier to copy.

To decorate a wooden or MDF base with imitation wood effects, the surfaces must be prepared with sealing primer; other kinds of base (walls, canvas, gypsum) should equally be made ready using the respective preparation techniques. In an inlay decoration or imitation wood lambris, it is best to follow the entire procedure described in the chapter dealing with masking and stencils.

WHAT'S NEEDED

Bucket, paper plates, paper tape, cutter, sponge, wave-effect stamp, combs, water-based and acrylic paints, boar and ox bristle brushes, retouching brushes in various sizes in synthetic sable, lilly bristle brush or jamb duster, flogger brush in mane bristle

A number of essential tools for imitation wood decorations
1- flogger brush
2- lilly bristle brush or jamb duster
3- wave-effect stamp
4- combs of various kinds and sizes

As regards colours, it is a good idea to have a sample ready at hand so that the exact colour shades of the wood can be reproduced; the shading can always be modified.

In all wood decorations, the technique involves two separate and very important parts. First and foremost, work must be performed rapidly since the imitation process is achieved while the paint is still wet or moist and acrylic and water-based paints dry very quickly; once the paint is dry, mistakes (unless minimal) cannot be corrected.

The first coat is used to give the lighter shade of the wood, i.e. the base visible through the veining, and has a major influence on the final result.

All woods can be given slightly different colours: more or less light (adding yellow, never white), yellower (less ochre) or pinker (a dash of red oxide); the shade must therefore be selected very carefully, performing several colour tests.

To avoid spoiling the colour and thus ruining the entire decoration the second stage is begun only when the base coat is thoroughly dry. The colours used in this stage must be highly diluted, almost veil-like, and before applying them, the underlying surface should be well moistened.

If the outcome is unsatisfactory, it is best to remove the paint immediately with a sponge and repeat the operation as preferred.

There is no room for hesitation: brush strokes must be continuous. The brush stroke can be repeated to spread the colour more evenly only if the paint is still wet.

Once dry, the shade of the wood effect can be modified by veiling but the veining cannot be changed. For finishing, in the case of an ornament or small object, two or three coats of water-based lacquer and two coats of wax are advisable; for surfaces subject to wear and tear, matt turpentine-based lacquers are preferable, although they do tend to yellow with age, because they do not interfere with the decoration.

Refer to specific indications for finishing methods for walls and other materials.

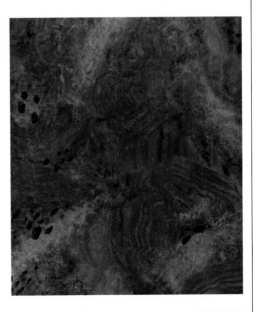

A box in ordinary wood can be transformed into a highly prized material such as briar.
Even the colour can be different: right: the colour shades of mahogany briar; opposite: maple wood effect.

WALNUT

The wood made from the walnut tree is veined, compact, hard and very well suited to processing and turning. Thanks to these features, walnut has always been used to make furniture, for veneering and highly prized flooring.
It is often imitated in trompe l'oeil, for bookcases, imitation picture frames, fittings and floors.

1- Having moistened the surface, apply colour A (somewhat diluted) with a brush, achieving a good coverage. The strokes must be uniform and applied in the same direction, without interrupting movement.

2- Wait until this colour is completely dry, the next step would be compromised if it is

1

2

3

4

WHAT'S NEEDED

Colours:
1-yellow, 2-ochre, 3-black, 4-red oxide, 5-umber, 6-sienna
Colour A-yellow plus ochre
Colour B-sienna plus red oxide plus umber
Colour C: umber plus black

Materials:
sponge, boar bristle brushes, flogger brush in mane bristle, lilly bristle brush or jamb duster

still moist. Then moisten the surface with a sponge.

3- Having prepared colours B and C, dilute them significantly so that the base colour shows through. Dip the brush in the paint and remove the excess water with a paper towel; begin applying colours B and C in the same direction as colour A. Interrupt the application of colour B to alternate it with small amounts of colour C which is used to paint the darker shades of the wood.

4- With a dry, clean

HINTS AND TIPS

When speaking of colours, it is taken for granted that they can be modified to suit personal preferences by altering colour components to achieve the required shade, which in wood can change, however slightly.

and very hard brush, "pull" the colour just applied before it dries completely, holding the brush as shown in the photograph in order to vary pressure and create areas where the colour is "pulled" differently than in others. The movement of the brush must be

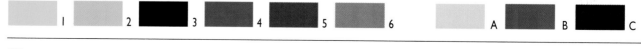

| | | | | | | | | |
|1|2|3|4|5|6|A|B|C|

5

6

Pale walnut, which has a rather golden colour, has little dark lines. To imitate these lines, treat the still moist surface of the decoration with a flogger brush dipped lightly in a little diluted umber.

7

8

constant and continuous over the length of the surface to be decorated. Eliminate excess colour with a paper towel and "pull" the colour again in the adjacent area, always in the same direction. The brush can be passed over more than once to achieve the required shading, provided the colour is still moist; as soon as you feel that the brush moves less easily, it means that the colour is drying and the work must be interrupted.

5- Before the paint is completely dry, pass a flogger brush (a very special brush found only in well-supplied art shops); this creates small lines, similar to the fibres of wood, through which the base colour can be seen. The moister the colour, the more evident this effect.

6- Immediately after this, prepare the decoration with a mane bristle brush or jamb duster (a very soft brush in badger bristle, also found in good art shops). Lightly touch the still moist surface with the mane bristle brush or jamb duster to

amalgamate the colours, creating an effect of the wood's natural compactness.

7- Apply two or three coats of water-based lacquer or turpentine-based matt lacquer as required.

8- Complete the decoration with two or three coats of wax to achieve a more natural effect.

Imitation walnut is often used in trompe l'oeil to paint frames.

MAHOGANY

A highly prized, hard and compact wood with a reddish colour which can be polished. Mahogany was very popular in neo-classic furniture designs, since it provided an excellent base for severe decoration involving engraving, inlays or gilt bronze fittings.
This effect, as for walnut, is widely used in wall decorations.

1- Apply colour A with a brush, having first moistened the surface, with a regular movement, always "pulling" the paint in the same direction so that brush strokes remain in evidence.

WHAT'S NEEDED

Colours:
1-lemon yellow,
2-red, 3-umber,
4-red oxide.
Colour A-lemon yellow plus a dash of red
Colour B-umber plus red oxide

Materials:
sponge, boar bristle brush, lilly bristle brush or jamb duster

2- When colour A is fully dry, apply diluted colour B over the surface (moistened with the sponge in advance).
Follow the direction of the underlying coat, without applying too much paint since the base must be visible.

3- Before this coat dries, quickly pass over the clean, moist sponge with the most jagged part on the wood and, in the same direction as above, "pull" the colour to form evident stripes.
The movement must be regular and continuous over the entire surface, without

interruptions.
Do not hesitate and remember that the larger the surface, the more quickly this operation has to be performed since the paint dries fast.

1   2   3   4   A   B

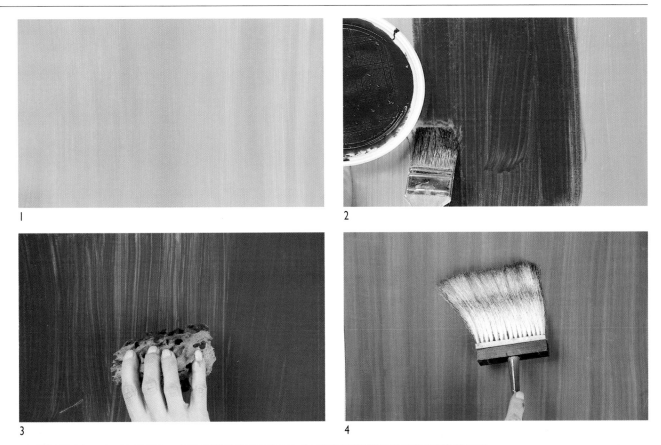

1

2

3

4

5

4- Before the paint is completely dry, pass over with the lily bristle brush or jamb duster, always following the direction of the veins.

5- As for all imitation wood effects, two or three coats of matt water-based lacquer (or spirit of turpentine) and two or three coats of wax achieve an ideal finish. For small objects in common wood a shiny gel can be used, since mahogany can be very bright even in its natural state.

Opposite: the decorative effect obtained with imitation mahogany is ideal for framing large bookcases.
Right: adding a touch of class to any room.

PALISSANDER

Indian palissander, also known as "bois de rose" or rosewood, was highly prized by French wood carvers in the 18ᵗʰ century.
It is a hard, strong wood which is still very popular today.
Less suited than mahogany for trompe l'oeil effects in view of its much darker colour and the more complicated reproduction technique, it is nevertheless ideal for decorating objects in ordinary wood.

1- Moisten the surface and apply diluted colour A with a brush. It doesn't matter if brush strokes are visible, it is important however that they are in the same direction.

I

2

WHAT'S NEEDED

Colours:
1-lemon yellow,
2-red, 3-black,
4-umber,
5-red oxide
Colour A-lemon yellow plus red
Colour B-umber plus black plus red oxide
Colour C-colour B plus black

Materials:
bristle brush, 3 and 4 mm flat brushes, 6 and 8 mm retouching brushes, flogger brush

2- When the surface is properly dry, dilute colour C somewhat and paint in the large dark veins typical of this wood over the moistened surface.

3- As soon as the veins are dry, apply diluted colour B with a brush so that the veins just painted and the base colour are still visible. "Pull" the colour with the brush so that the underlying colours are more apparent in certain areas,

thereby creating lighter shades.

4- When the surface is dry, use colour B and a retouching brush, moistening the base from time to time, to intensify the shade in certain areas, creating thinner veins with the same patterning.

5- Wait until all the veining effects are dry and, dipping the flogger brush lightly into colour B, dab the entire dry surface with

small, fast dabs to design the fibres of the wood.

6- Palissander, like mahogany, can be polished more than other woods; consequently, over and above water-based and matt turpentine-based lacquers and waxes, shiny gel is equally an ideal finish for objects decorated in this manner.

I   2   3   4   5   A   B   C

3

4

5

6

Imitation palissander decoration was used for the base of a gilt candelabra and small photograph frames.

BRIAR

Briar is a commonly used term but, in reality, it should be preceded by the wood of its origin - since briars can be obtained from walnut, cherry, mahogany and so forth. Briar characterized by veins and numerous knots is the wood made from the roots of trees.
The shades of colour, the veining and the position of the knots all depend on the wood of origin.
The reproduction technique is the same for all briars - only the colours and the knot patterns change.

If you want to imitate a specific briar, then it is essential to have a sample ready to hand.

Left: a papier mâché box can become a lovely ornament if decorated well in imitation briar (above).

WHAT'S NEEDED

Colours:
1-lemon yellow,
2-red, 3-umber,
4-sienna, 5-red oxide,
6-ochre
Colour A-lemon yellow plus red oxide or ochre
Colour B-umber plus sienna
Colour C-umber plus sienna plus red oxide or ochre

Materials:
sponge, bristle brush, 4 and 6 mm retouching brushes in synthetic sable or ox bristle, card (see Malachite)

Highly decorative, imitation briar can be used to decorate objects in ordinary wood, small objects in papier mâché, wood inlays, small items of furniture, ornaments and lampshades. Different amounts of the various components provide the colour shades typical of the various types of wood.

1- Dilute colour A somewhat so that it resembles the natural colouring of the briar; this will be more or less orange depending on the amounts of red and ochre used.
The colour should then be applied to the moistened surface with irregular, curved strokes.

2- When the surface is dry, colour B (not particularly diluted but of varying intensity) can be used to draw the knots with a retouching brush. Copy the patterns of the sample, modifying the size and, if necessary, the intensity of the colour and shape, which should be more or less rounded. The smaller knots can be fuller and darker in colour, whereas the larger ones should resemble paler, concentric circles.

3- Once the knots are dry, use a clean sponge to moisten the surface and immediately move onto the next step. Prepare the required shade of colour C, dilute it significantly and test it in a corner to see if it gives the right effect when sponged onto colour A; if not, immediately sponge off and darken with a little umber or lighten with ochre or yellow depending on the required effect (red oxide is used in both cases to match the colour with the red).

1   2   3   4   5   6

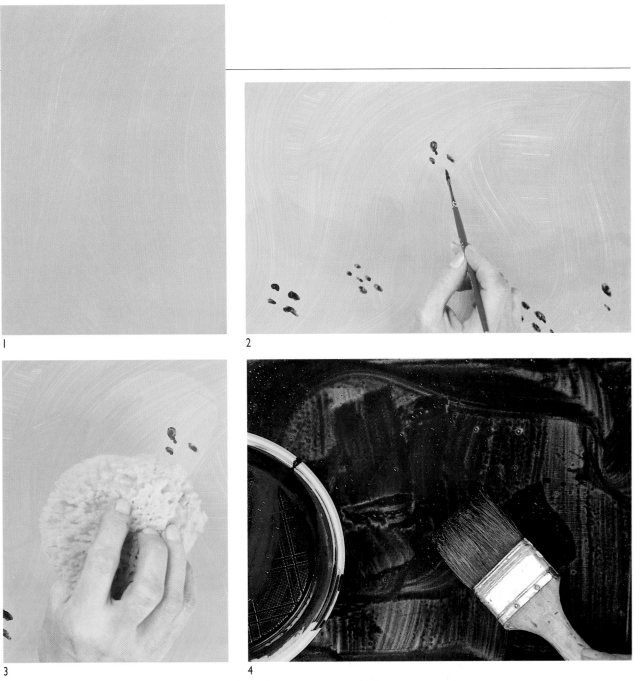

1

2

3

4

4- Apply the colour to the moist surface with a brush; it should not provide too much coverage since the underlying base must remain visible. Try to follow the stripes painted previously with colour A.

5- Before the colour dries, use a clean, moist sponge to remove a little in certain places and around the knots, so that lighter areas are created in which the base is more evident.

5

A   B   C

6- Moisten the surface again and pass over with a dry boar bristle brush with curved movements, especially near the groups of knots, to create stripes. Knotting can be very apparent in some kinds of briar. In such cases, use a card in place of the brush (as for Malachite decoration). The movement, however, is less complicated than that needed for Malachite "roses". You can interrupt the action, or create any more or less circular pattern, and it is possible to correct mistakes or lumps of colour by passing a sponge over them.

7- Briar decorations are the only ones of this kind which permit errors to be corrected once the paint is dry. Errors cannot be eliminated quickly in any other imitation wood technique. In this case - without damaging the decoration and retaining a natural effect - it is possible to sponge over the area to be corrected with colour C (not very dilute) to mask the mistake.
The ideal finish for briar is water-based or matt turpentine-based lacquer, together with wax, as described elsewhere.

6

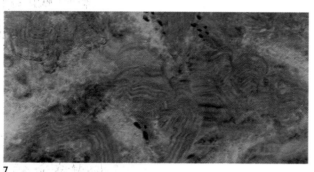

7

Above: example of imitation maple briar decoration.
Side: a very unusual jewellery box decorated in imitation mahogany briar.

PINE

Pine is undoubtedly the wood most commonly used for inexpensive, popular and rustic furniture. It is not particularly hard and has a low impact strength and since it has many knots and veins, it is not suited to turning work, because it easily splinters.
It can be used with excellent results in carpentry for beams, uprights and so forth. Obviously, the colour changes in relation to the kind of pine used (white or red), covering a range from beige to light yellow. One or two coats of water-based lacquer are sufficient to protect the paint once finished. Colours and materials must be distinguished in relation to the type of decoration: the rustic style reproduces new panelling made with boards of pine, whereas it may be preferable to imitate beams aged with the passing of time.

Left: imitation beams painted with the trompe l'oeil effect resembling aged pine. Above: imitation panelling in a room decorated to resemble young pine.

1

Pine wall panelling

Decorations in imitation pine are generally used to embellish walls.

1- Moisten the surface and use the brush to apply diluted colour A. "Pull" it to leave evident brush strokes which should be parallel over the entire surface.

2- Dilute colour B and wait until the surface is completely dry, then moisten it and apply the colour with the brush, following the direction of the underlying coat.

3- Before the colour dries, use the wave-effect block (easy to find in Britain, less so elsewhere) and "pull" the colour, oscillating

2

somewhat to form concentric ellipses similar to the veins in wood. To close the pattern, slowly return the tool to the starting point. The more slowly the hand zigzags in relation to the "pull" of the colour (i.e. as the hand slides along the surface in the direction of the brush strokes), the more elongated the ellipses; the quicker the movement, the shorter the ellipses. Before attempting this kind of decoration, it is a good idea to practise to learn how to synchronize the two movements and adjust pressure in order to obtain the required effect.

4- Before colour B alongside the veins just formed dries, "pull" it with one side of the wave-effect tool used above. The two sides have combs of different sizes (in this instance, use the larger toothed comb). It is also possible to use combs available in well-supplied ironmongers in various sizes. Depending on the size of the teeth, more or less separated veins can be reproduced. Pull the comb or the tool with a constant movement, always parallel to the brush stroke.

WHAT'S NEEDED

Colours:
1-white, 2-lemon yellow, 3-ochre, 4-red oxide, 5-sienna
Colour A-lemon yellow plus ochre plus a dash of white
Colour B-ochre plus a dash of red oxide and sienna
Colour C-colour B plus another dash of sienna

Materials:
bristle brush, wave-effect block or combs, lilly bristle brush or jamb duster, 6 mm synthetic sable retouching brush

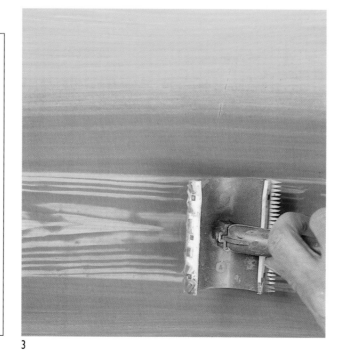

3

| | 1 | | 2 | | 3 | | 4 | | 5 | | A | | B | | C |

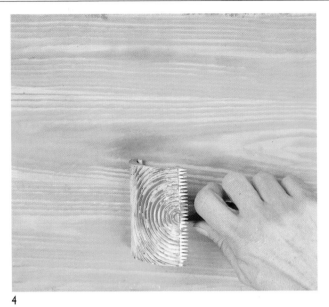

4

5

5- Use the lilly bristle or jamb duster brush on the still moist paint to amalgamate the veins and achieve the natural compactness of wood.

6- When the paint is dry, use rather diluted colour C to paint knots with the retouching brush.
Don't forget to moisten the underlying surface so that the paint runs naturally; brush with circular strokes so that different colour shades are formed inside the knot.

7- It is extremely important not to design knots all of the same size but distinguish them over the whole surface in terms of both number and position. To protect the decoration, apply one or two coats of water-based lacquer.

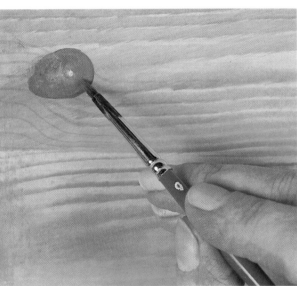

6

7

Aged pine

If you want to depict greying old beams, the base must be a wall, a canvas or MDF panels prepared with two coats of water-based primer.

1- Having first moistened the surface with a wet sponge, apply colour A (diluted) with regular brush strokes (all in the same direction), trying not to break the stroke for the whole length of the beam itself.

2- Once the paint is dry, use very diluted colour B to draw in veins of various sizes with a retouching brush, using a paint-spotted sponge here and there to simulate the marks left in wood by wear and tear. Remember to moisten the surface from time to time before painting the veins. Before the colour dries, pass over the veins quickly with

I

2

WHAT'S NEEDED

Colours:
1-white, 2-umber, 3-black, 4-ochre, 5-red oxide
Colour A-white plus umber and ochre
Colour B-umber plus black
Colour C-umber plus very little red oxide and ochre

Materials:
bristle brush, 4 and 8 mm synthetic sable retouching brushes, lilly bristle brush or jamb duster

the lilly bristle brush or jamb duster in the same direction as the first coat to blur the edges.

3- When the surface is completely dry, moisten it again and then apply very dilute colour C with a brush, always following the same brush stroke direction along the beam. "Pull" the colour fully so that it appears almost like a veil through which the veins are perfectly visible. Before the colour dries

completely, dab lightly with the lilly bristle brush or jamb duster to cancel brush strokes and amalgamate the top coat with the base coat for a more realistic appearance.
Protect the decoration with one or two coats of matt water-based lacquer.

Opposite page, bottom: examples of pine decoration using the trompe l'oeil technique. Top right: a detailed enlargement.

| | I | | 2 | | 3 | | 4 | | 5 | | A | | B | | C |

3

STENCILS

An ancient decorative art, stencils make it possible to reproduce designs on various kinds of surface, such as paper, textiles, wood and walls. Stencils are cut-out designs in card, metal or other materials (such as acetate or manilla paper) through which the colour is dabbed so that the design is transferred onto the underlying surface through the cut-outs.

Items have been found in China in paper and silk decorated with the stencil technique dating from 3000 B.C. English churches dating from the 13th-14th centuries still display decorations made in this manner and, in Tudor England, many decorators used stencils on plain white walls.

With the arrival from China of wall paper at the end of the 17th century decorative taste passed over to these more sophisticated products and stencil-work was soon forgotten: it was used only in places where wallpaper was hard to find or very expensive such as America. This is one of the reasons why stencil-work is associated with the early American colonists, who took the technique with them from Europe.

Designs were inspired by the typical motifs of different countries in different periods. The Dutch preferred designs based on tulips, leaves and hearts, the Americans those inspired by Indian culture; stencil decoration of the Victorian and Second Empire period involved garlands of fruit and flowers. The Liberty and Art Deco period made extensive use of print painting techniques and took up all the motifs best suited to this new taste.

Simplicity of execution and enormous versatility helped further broaden the popularity of stencil-work, which became a decorative method still very much in vogue today, especially in other fields such as Country decoration, in which the same design is repeated many times.

Opposite: detail of a wall decorated with stencil motifs. Above: a lampshade in plain linen. Both are decorated with damask designs of the Victorian age.

Panel with a cornice and figures reproduced using stencils.
Below: a detailed enlargement of the cornice.

The designs on this page are examples of stencils inspired by a variety of decorative styles.

Above: screen decorated with damask designs painted using the stencil technique.

Stencils can be used in various ways but the difficulty of execution (excepting the time needed to complete the task) is always the same, whether decorating a small object or an entire wall. Stencil-work decorations can also highlight existing architectural elements or hide irregularities. A ceiling which seems too high can be "lowered" by inserting a stencil border 10-20 cm (4-8 in) below it; long, narrow corridors can be "shortened" with motifs that follow vertical lines; windows and small, insignificant niches can be emphasized by appropriate stencil-work. It is important to select the

Left: the drawings show
how light and shade
effects give stencil-work
the depth of inlays.
Below: a tray decorated
with small love-knots
made using stencils and
repeated in the corners.

design in relation to the overall shape of
the room; in a very irregular room, it is
better to choose open motifs which
distract attention from the general form
of the room itself. For staircases, it is
best to avoid oblique lines, since
it is extremely difficult to give them
the same angle as the stairs. It isn't
necessary to do complicated things -
even a simple design in a single colour
can be embellished with small touches
of light and shade (as explained in the
décor chapter); but it is essential that
the motifs selected blend harmoniously
with the room. You can copy the design
of curtains and repeat it as a border
around the walls of a room or,
otherwise, a decorative element existing
in the room can be used to brighten
curtains, tablecloths or quilts.
For the first attempt at stencil-work, it is
advisable to select a very simple design
which is easy to transform into a stencil.
Having cut out the windows and the
bridges (the former as the "holes"
through which the colour passes, the
latter the connecting parts which
remain blank), the paint is
then dabbed onto the surface
(which should always be
prepared in advance with a
white or coloured water-based
paint).

A floral cornice painted
20 cm (8 in) below the
ceiling helps harmonize
the dimensions of a room.
Below: a repetitive motif
transformed into a stencil.
Applied as many times as
necessary, it can frame
and decorate any object.

STENCILS ON WOOD

The surface on which the decoration is to be made must be in good condition and clean; the base must be suitably prepared. The first time you undertake stencil work, it is a good idea to practise on a piece of wood prepared in the same way as the base to be decorated to gain experience and control chromatic effects. Also make sure that the various materials are compatible with each other when deciding to make a stencil of an existing base. Water-based paints, earths and acrylic paints are generally always compatible with each other.

The selected design must be enlarged or reduced directly onto the acetate. If a mistake is made while cutting out the stencil, it can be corrected by applying paper tape to both sides.

The same technique is used to repair a stencil which has broken through use, however it is advisable to prepare two copies of the stencil if the area to be decorated is rather large.

Before starting the task, it is a good idea to protect the floor with sheets of newspaper and prepare all necessary materials.

Don't forget a bucket of water and paper towels to remove excess paint from the brushes.

One brush is needed for each colour, to avoid having to wash (and therefore dry) brushes during stencil-work.

The paint should not be too dilute, except as required to amalgamate the colours, since they must provide good coverage.

1- Prepare the materials required for

WHAT'S NEEDED

Colours:
1-white, 2-blue,
3-black, 4-green,
5-ochre
Colour A-white plus blue plus black
Colour B-colour A plus white
Colour C-green plus ochre plus black
Colour D-colour C plus ochre

Materials:
tracing paper, pencil, eraser, pencil-sharpener, paper tape, acetate (manilla paper or even a plastic folder), coloured indelible felt-tip pens, cutter (or pyrograph cutter), a piece of glass, card or wood panel to protect the work surface, stencil brushes, sponge

1	2	3	4	5

2

3

4

5

6

the task: tracing paper, acetate, eraser, pencil and felt-tip pens.

2- Transfer the design onto paper.

3- Transform this design into a stencil by marking out the windows and bridges.

4- Transfer the design onto the acetate, using felt-tip pens of different colours for the windows which will be painted with the same colour (blue and green).
Bear in mind that when working with stencils having more than one

colour, as many stencils have to be prepared as colours and each one will have cut-out windows for the particular colour.

5 & 6- To cut acetate, you can use a normal cutter or an electrical pyrograph,

like those used to mark leather or wood. In this case, it is advisable to protect the work table with a piece of glass.

A   B   C   D

7- Before starting the stencilling task, it is a good idea to centre the design using a ruler or a set-square and mark the surface with a pencil through the register.

8- To secure the stencil, use spray glue (used by graphic artists because the design can be repositioned) or paper tape. It is important that the stencil doesn't move while applying the colour.

7

HINTS AND TIPS

If the stencil design involves more than one colour (photograph below) a register mark is made on each stencil to ensure that they are properly aligned. Proceed as follows: having cut out the various stencils and aligned them so that the various parts are in the correct position, trim the edges so that every stencil has the same dimensions. Leaving them on top of each other, cut out two

small register windows in all stencils, one top right and the other bottom left.
Before starting to stencil, mark the surface to be decorated with a pencil through the registers, making sure that the marks overlap properly each time a stencil is positioned; this ensures perfect alignment.

A cornice and its stencil with the positioning register.

8

9

It is important to dose the colour well in stencil-work. Depending on the amount used, the edges may be irregular (1) or very pale (2). Edges will be clear and regular (3) only if an almost dry brush is used and provided the colour does not penetrate underneath the stencil.

1

2   3

9- Dip the flogger brush into the green paint so that it penetrates well into the bristles; eliminate the excess (too much paint can cause ragged edges) by dabbing the brush against a paper towel until only a slight shadow of paint is applied.
Dab on the paint holding the brush vertically over the surface, with rapid movements of constant pressure, starting from the edges of the windows and moving towards the centre. To achieve different shading effects, do not increase the pressure but repeat the dabbing operation in the areas which are to be darker. Remove the stencil and wait until the colour dries completely before positioning the next stencil.

When placing the second stencil, make sure the register marks line up. In this example, two shades of sky blue were used (modifying the amount of blue). Since the two colours are very similar, the same brush can be used. Remember to dab on the lighter colour first, clean and dry the brush and then dab on the second colour. Varnish can be applied to the finished decoration to protect it.

Once finished, the chair harmonizes perfectly with the decoration of the room which was copied to prepare the stencil.

STENCIL ON FABRIC

Coloured dyes suitable for fabric stencils are available commercially in good art shops. If you want to decorate a tablecloth or a table centrepiece, which will inevitably be washed frequently, it is best to use these colours, even if they are more expensive than water-based paint, since they are more durable. The technique doesn't change.

If the object to be decorated will not be washed very often (such as a lampshade), a good water-based paint suffices to obtain a durable decoration. In both cases, only natural fabrics should be used (such as linen or cotton) and should be washed and ironed beforehand, so that there are no creases which would otherwise interfere with the stencil work.

Top: a curtain decorated with the same design as a bedspread; top right: detail of the decoration. Right: the materials needed, pencil, eraser, felt-tip pen, cutter, paper towels, repositionable spray glue, acetate, copy paper, ruler, paints, flogger brush in mane bristle, stencil.

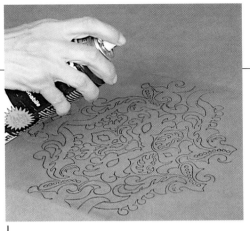

1- Arrange the necessary materials and, if a specific motif is to be transformed into a stencil to be reproduced on a curtain, everything needed must be ready at hand. These materials include acetate, cutter, copy paper, ruler, pencil, eraser and indelible felt-tip pen.
Spray the glue on the stencil as already described. If the fabric is very lightweight, it is best to place it on a paper cloth to absorb any excess paint which may pass through the fibres.

2- Dip the brush in the colour and dab it on a piece of paper towel to remove the excess.

3- Begin dabbing the fabric.

4- Compared with stencil work on walls or wood, fabrics are much easier. The colour is absorbed immediately without forming rough edges.

The decorative motif of the eiderdown was repeated here on a lampshade.

RUSTIC PAINTING

Ataste for decoration has always been natural to mankind and, depending on the time and place, various styles of decoration have been developed over time. Each one has been distinguished by the materials, techniques and decorative motifs employed.

Rustic painting, like Country and Tyrolean décor or découpage, is a very simple form of decoration generally used with walls or furniture and developed essentially in the countryside and small towns. It is characterized by simple decorations, fast and easy execution and the use of ordinary materials, unlike more refined decorative techniques such as trompe l'oeil, grisaille and imitation marble.

Rustic decoration is an art form linked closely with the culture and preferences of its place of origin. Interest in this art form over the years has become so deep-rooted that nowadays, decorators use specific techniques for base decoration such as scratched varnish and aged wood, in order to achieve the effect of an old rustic motif.

The materials required include acrylic paints, sponges and brushes, as well as everything else needed to reproduce the design. Moreover, an antiquating patina and glass paper are also needed to "age" the decoration and water-based lacquers and waxes to protect it.

Colour shades in rustic decoration tend to be dark, since in the past the colours generally used were black and darker shades of red, blue and green. This was because in the absence of specific colour fixing products these colours were longer-lasting once painted onto wood.

Opposite: a trellis and climbing plants.
Above: a table top with a country decoration recalling patchwork fabric motifs.

Above: a simple casket transformed into an heirloom thanks to Country décor.

There is a great deal of room for personal creativity in Country décor, taking inspiration from the various colours and styles of different countries such as Mexico, Africa and the Slav nations. Geometrical patterns, in particular, are well-suited when decorating objects of regular shape, such as boxes and cornices. The dimensions of floral decorations should be adapted to the size of the surface being decorated. Specialist books and magazines, as well as motifs copied from fabrics, are an important and essential source of inspiration.

Above: decorative motifs typical of rustic painting.
Left: a simple wardrobe of the early 1800s from Val Badia, Italy.

The floral motif of the curtains was used to create a border around the ceiling cornice in this room.

COUNTRY DECOR

This kind of decoration, characterized by the simplicity and freshness of the colours used, is popular in Great Britain and France, especially in Provence. Many motifs used in this technique are inspired by Dutch traditions (tulips, leaves, garlands and bows) and those of the American Indians. Items of rustic furniture are best suited to this kind of decoration but Country décor is equally appealing with small objects. An enormous variety of motifs can be used such as floral, classic scrolls and small cornices. Country décor, first and foremost, requires the drawing to be transferred onto the pre-prepared surface

using graphite paper; the flowers and leaves are then painted in, followed by light and shade effects.
If a wooden or composite wood object is to be painted, the preparation of the base depends on the condition of the article. If it is in good condition, two or three coats of water-based primer will suffice, followed by a good glass-papering; if the

natural colour of the item of furniture does not interfere with the shade selected for the decoration, two or three coats of filler can be applied.
In relation to base decoration, mordants can also be used, as well as the "scratched varnish" technique and sponging with a uniform colour, in order to enhance the final decoration. For the inside segments,

the same treatments as for the outside can be used such as mordants or aged wood finishing. For finishing, it is advisable to use two or three coats of matt water-based lacquer, followed by a coat of wax.
Stencils are ideally suited to the Country style, especially when combining the technique with hand pictorial painting. They speed up the process of applying the repetitive motifs characteristic of Country décor, while hand-painted elements are used to set off the decoration, making it less static.

Top: the decorative motif of fabric used to decorate a plain wooden base of a lamp.
Right: highlights given to a bunch of flowers painted uniformly to start with.

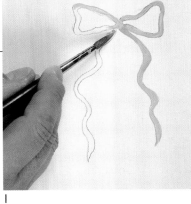

1

2

3

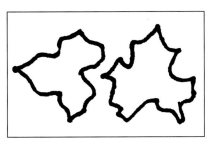

4

Country décor and small objects

A wastepaper bin in bare wood was glass-papered, painted with two coats of water-based protective primer and finished with beige water-paint in two different shades applied simultaneously to the surface with clearly visible brush strokes.

1- When the surface is dry, design a bow (or transfer it with copy paper) and paint it with a synthetic sable retouching brush of suitable dimensions.

2- Using a 2 mm synthetic sable retouching brush, paint in the twigs, having first marked them out with a hard pencil, using water-colour paint. The colouring should be uneven.

3- Position acetate stencils with simple ivy leaf cut-outs at random near the twigs and complete the decoration by dabbing on the selected colour.

4- Having completed this task, paint in the stems linking the leaves to the twigs and the small berries. Use retouching brushes of suitable size. Repeat the procedure on each side of the wasterpaper bin. Two or three coats of matt water-based lacquer should be applied to finish.

Above: detail of the stencil of the ivy leaves used to complete the decoration. This simple motif, repeated on any object, ensures that it fits in well with any kind of Country décor.

Country décor and large surfaces

The same technique used for small objects can easily be used to decorate much larger surfaces such as cupboards very quickly. The outside and inside of the cupboard can be treated with three base coats of water-based primer to whiten the colour and make the surface smoother.

1

2

1- Prepare two different stencils: the first is a simple, geometric cornice, the other a combination of small leaves and berries following the outline of the cornice.

2- Using two colours, different bases and different stencil positions, even a large piece of furniture can be decorated harmoniously, thereby distinguishing the various parts. For example, an even sky blue base (mixing blue, white and black) can alternate with a pale beige base sponged lightly with ochre so that it is not too intense.

3- On the sky blue base: darken the basic colour by adding more blue and a little black and then stencil in the small leaves, which can later be joined together by a long twig painted free-hand with a retouching brush.

4- On the beige base: use the same colour as the sponging to stencil in the geometric cornice.

3

4

5

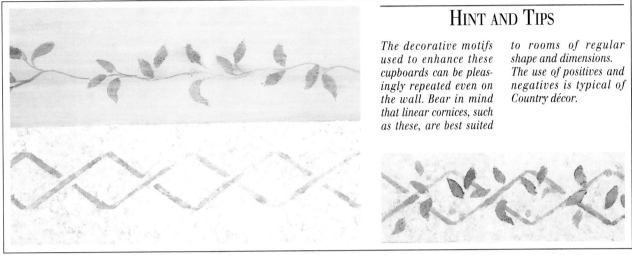

HINT AND TIPS

The decorative motifs used to enhance these cupboards can be pleasingly repeated even on the wall. Bear in mind that linear cornices, such as these, are best suited to rooms of regular shape and dimensions. The use of positives and negatives is typical of Country décor.

5- You can also use the small leaf stencil to decorate the cornice surrounding the glass doors, thereby highlighting them in contrast with the lower cupboards.
Finish the decoration with two or three covering coats of water-based lacquer.

A rather ordinary set of cupboards can be made unique by decorating the frames of the doors and drawers with Country motifs using stencils.

Kitchen furniture

A piece of furniture decorated in the rustic style for inclusion in a kitchen. Using umber instead of antiquating patina, the factory-new cupboard takes on the appearance of a fine old dresser.

1- Having prepared the base of the item of furniture with three coats of filler, apply two covering coats of not too diluted water-paint. In the first instance it was decided to use two different shades of beige for the small cornices but having painted on the stencil work the result was not contrasting enough and the darker beige was replaced by penicillin green (made by mixing green, black, ochre and white). Since the colours are not very dilute and thus provide reasonably good coverage, it is possible

to apply another colour on top of a neutral shade such as off-white or beige. This achieves the natural effect typical of this kind of decoration.

2- The stencil used was developed from a free-hand drawing which was transferred onto tracing paper and then

made into a stencil, marking the windows and bridges, before being cut out on a sheet of acetate.

3- Dab the non-diluted ochre water paint onto

the door; without removing the stencil, dab absolute white in certain parts to shade the colouring of the leaves.

4- When the paint is completely dry, use a retouching brush and a little ochre, red oxide and green to touch up in certain points.

HINTS AND TIPS

Colour can be applied (as in this case) with a dry natural sponge dipped in the paint and then wiped on a paper towel to remove the excess in place of flogger brushes. Hold the sponge firmly between your fingers and dab the colour lightly onto the stencil. In general, it is preferable to use a sponge instead of a flogger brush when the stencil decoration is to be applied to a rather large surface area. It is a lot quicker and produces a more blurred and irregular colour when required.

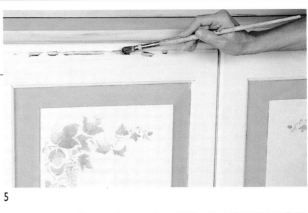

5

4

6

Highlight the stems with green, intensify the colours of some leaves with very dilute red oxide, retouch the bunches of grapes and use ochre to highlight the outline of one or two leaves.

5- Wait until the paint is completely dry and then use very dilute umber in place of antiquating patina to "dust down" the decoration so that it seems more like an old dresser than something just delivered from a modern factory.

6- Moisten the surface with a sponge and use a stub brush to dab diluted paint into the parts where dirt accumulates more easily and where normal wear and tear is frequent. Use the moist sponge quickly to "pull" this colour until the required effect is obtained.
Repeat the operation where necessary.
Protect the decoration

with several coats of water-based lacquer.

An old cupboard, cleaned and decorated, can now grace any lounge.

TYROLEAN DECOR

A typical kind of rustic painting is the Tyrolean style with rustic and floral decorations popular in northern Europe. The Tyrolean style in Italy developed mainly in the Tyrol (hence the name); decorative elements and application techniques have remained largely unchanged over time, so much so that one can even trace the country of origin from the type of design. This kind of decoration is made exclusively on wooden furniture such as doors and panelled

*Top: characteristic decorations of the 1800s: left: roses and tulips in a floral composition enhanced by a vase decorated in the grisaille style; centre: friezes and scrolls typical of north European decorations; right: garlands of tulips and roses.
Right: simple flowers typical of Tyrolean decoration.*

WHAT'S NEEDED

Colours:
1-dusty blue,
2-penicillin green,
3-olive green,
4-dark red,
5-ultramarine

Materials:
glass-paper, paper tape, sponge, bristle brushes, graphite paper, retouching brush in synthetic sable.

rooms. As a result, the preparation of the base is the same as for all woods. For the exterior, you can decide among several types of base (mordant, aged wood, scratched varnish or plain painting), whereas, for the inside, mordant or aged wood techniques are preferred.
The most commonly used colours are dusty blue, penicillin green, olive green, dark red and ultramarine blue.

After applying two coats of water-based lacquer, wax is used for finishing off.
Antiquating patinas are also often used in this kind of decoration.
Since Tyrolean décor is characterized by a

| | 1 | | 2 | | 3 | | 4 | | 5 |

Left: a two-piece dresser from the north Tyrol (Elbach) dating from the early 1800s in a Baroque-like style.
This page: examples of typical Tyrolean decorative elements.

strict decorative style, it is advisable to prepare an accurate plan not only of the design itself but also of the colour scheme before beginning the task. In fact, errors cannot be rectified in this technique and it is not possible to modify or change colours without damaging the natural appearance of the decoration.

This design was made by copying the décor of period furniture and then combining different elements to create an original composition.

Tyrolean linen chest

Embellishing a simple linen chest with Tyrolean décor is by no means an easy task since, unlike Country décor, it requires some degree of pre-planning.

1- First and foremost, take precise measurements of the inset panels which are to be decorated and mark out a draft with the typical ornamental motifs of Tyrolean décor, adapting them to these dimensions.

2- Having selected the kind of décor (taking inspiration from classic motifs in books and magazines), make several photocopies so that the colours can be studied. Once you have chosen the base colour, it is a good idea to prepare a sample of the complete decoration on paper.

3- When you have completed the plan, work can begin. Apply two coats of covering water-based primer; the surface should be carefully glass-papered before and after.

4- With a not too dilute beige, fill in the central panels and add extra brush strokes here and there to create the "scratched varnish" appearance.

5- Wax the areas darkened with beige.

6- Use paper tape to mask the central panels; moisten the rest of the item with a

3

4

sponge, taking care not to touch the areas where wax was previously applied.

7- Prepare two shades of blue of different luminosity and apply these colours (not too dilute so that good coverage is achieved) with regular brush strokes in the same direction as the other parts of the chest. Use two different bristle brushes for the two colours in alternating sections, so that the outline of the chest is highlighted. Make sure that the two colours contrast distinctly; if the contrast is too slight, lighten one with white or darken the other with a little black. Apply the colour carefully to the waxed areas.

5

6

7

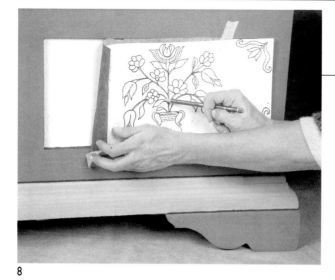

8

9

10

11

12

13

8- Transfer the design using graphite paper.

9- Before beginning to paint the drawing, use a rag soaked in turpentine to remove the blue from the waxed sections and then sand lightly with glass-paper n. 230 to accompany the colour.

10 & 11- Use a retouching brush in synthetic sable of appropriate dimensions to begin decorating the various elements of the design with undiluted paints.

12- When the paint is completely dry, use a synthetic sable brush to accentuate highlights in some places by adding small touches of white.

13- Having finished the decoration, wait until the paintwork is completely dry and then protect with two coats of water-based matt lacquer.

14- Once the lacquer is dry, apply antiquating patina to the entire chest, "pulling" it irregularly with a paper towel to leave more product in the corners and in the grooves.
Before judging the final decoration, wait 24-48 hours until the patina is dry.

In typically Tyrolean style, this linen chest is ideally suited to the furnishing of a mountain home. Above: detail of the floral decoration.

14

DECOUPAGE

Around the mid 17th century, paper-cutting was considered an art in its own right, so much so that it was encouraged and included in the education of the daughters of the gentry just like painting and embroidery.

Although we cannot speak of true découpage as such, since in the past finishing lacquers applied to the glued figures were still not used, it was nevertheless a good beginning.

The fashion for "chinoiserie" gave rise to the taste for lacquered objects; French artists, in particular (découpage is French for "cutting out"), were the first to produce objects in the Chinese style and books were published with images to be cut out, glued and treated with gum lacquer. In

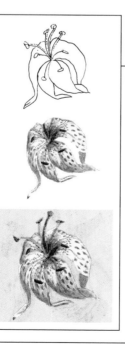

the 18th century, découpage found enthusiasts among kings, nobles and the middle classes throughout Europe and even spread to North America. The art went into decline when designs came to be produced which were already partly cut out and fell into disuse at the end of the Victorian age. Today, in view of the many kinds of lacquer available on the market, which make the task much quicker, and given the vast amount of reference material, découpage has become popular again. The results which can be obtained with this technique are aesthetically pleasing; subjects can be taken from all kinds of source: magazines, books and wallpaper. The selected images should be photocopied in colour in suitable dimensions. The base to which the figures will be affixed must be suitable for the subject and the colours. Excellent results can also be obtained by combining découpage with other decorative techniques, such as stencilling.

Even if this is an easy technique, certain aspects require close attention if optimal results are to be achieved. Firstly, bear in mind the thickness of the paper: if it is more than 0.2 mm thick, there is the risk of producing a relief effect; if it is thinner (copy paper) problems may arise when gluing it in place.

A good outcome also depends on how the figures are cut, since the margins should be very clear.

To cut out the subject, use nail scissors with curved tips (rotating them at the same time as turning the paper) and a cutter, to be used in the most complicated points. When using a cutter, it is best to rest the paper on glass to avoid spoiling the underlying surface.

A botanical print was glued to the wall and embellished with a trompe l'oeil frame.

HINTS AND TIPS

If the picture to be cut out has elements that are so small there is a risk of tearing it (like the stems of a flower), there are two possible solutions: leave a larger margin around the detail and then paint over it, or eliminate the part and repaint it in at the end directly onto the surface where the picture is glued.

2

3

4

5

6

1- A factory-new object, such as a base of a lamp, can be transformed using découpage into a unique and specific object to achieve a particular furnishing effect. Begin by applying two coats of water-based lacquer (whether the item already has a base coat of paint or if this coat has just been applied). Once dry, rub delicately with a moist n. 600 abrasive paper.

2- Having carefully cut out the selected image establish its exact position on the object.

3- Position the decoration on the surface and make reference marks with a pencil to avoid hesitation when gluing.

4- Place the image face down on a sheet of plastic and brush it with lacquer.

5- With great care (using tweezers if the figure is very small) position the decoration on the surface, also lacquered so that no creases are formed. Brush over the decoration with lacquer, pressing so that it adheres perfectly.

6- Remove excess lacquer with a moist cloth and press down carefully on the design with a roller; move from the centre outwards. To avoid the risk of damaging the decoration in this stage, a moist cloth can be placed between the roller and the figure. There must be no creases or air bubbles; if this is likely, because the figure is rather large, it is better to cut it in half and glue the two pieces separately. These guidelines are also applicable when making a découpage decoration on a wall.

The final effect on this wooden base of a lamp is by no means banal and gives no impression of being something copied and glued in place.

GRISAILLE

In the 17th century the fashion for trompe l'oeil became extremely popular among the middle classes of northern Europe and this form of decoration became increasingly common. This was largely for practical reasons. It was undoubtedly easier to paint an imitation cornice than carve it in wood, bearing in mind that Scandinavian wood is generally soft and therefore not easy to work.

At the same time, another kind of decoration came to the fore, grisaille. The stucco-work and carvings typical of the Baroque style thus came to be replaced by paintings which imitated their shapes and designs.

Grisaille was especially used to make friezes around a room, imitation panelling, low reliefs or imitation statues.

Grisaille decorations are monochromatic, i.e. they involve only one colour, generally grey (the term derives from *gris*, French for grey), used in various degrees of luminosity to create three-dimensional effects. As well as various shades of grey, colours such as brown, blue and green can also be used.

A good grisaille decoration requires excellent understanding of the technical principles of light and shade, which help make a flat surface seem three-dimensional; in a certain sense, it resembles the effect of trompe l'oeil.

First and foremost, start from the concept that an object exposed to light has an illuminated part and a shadowed part and that the object itself also throws a shadow onto the surface where it stands.

To give more depth to a decoration, you should assume that a source of light is placed next to and slightly above the object in question: front lighting tends to flatten forms and light coming from the side at the same height as the object would not highlight all parts in the same way. Since rays of light are parallel to each other, it is always preferable to imagine the sun as the source of light rather than a lamp.

A female figure decorated in the grisaille style is highlighted against an imitation "peperino" marble base.
Opposite: a low relief depicting three women created with the same technique.

*Right and below: the same "grisaille" image as before in different shades of grey.
Far right: the grisaille technique used to decorate an imitation frame around a trompe l'oeil; below: detail.*

The use of different shades has helped give this pedestal a three-dimensional appearance.

So, having determined the angle of illumination, it must remain the same for every part of the object.

To make a three-dimensional decoration, the object itself must be "imagined" in a three-dimensional way. It is therefore important to identify the following: the illuminated parts, i.e. those struck by the ray of light, and paint them with the lighter colour; the parts not struck perpendicularly by the light, which are painted in a medium colour; the shadow areas, painted in the darker colour. The parts in the shadow thrown by the object itself should be painted in a medium-dark colour.

To familiarize yourself with these concepts, the execution of a grisaille decoration must be followed step-by-step, carefully defining the details. The successful outcome of this kind of decoration depends entirely on starting from a perfect design of the image. If you decide to paint a cornice or frame in

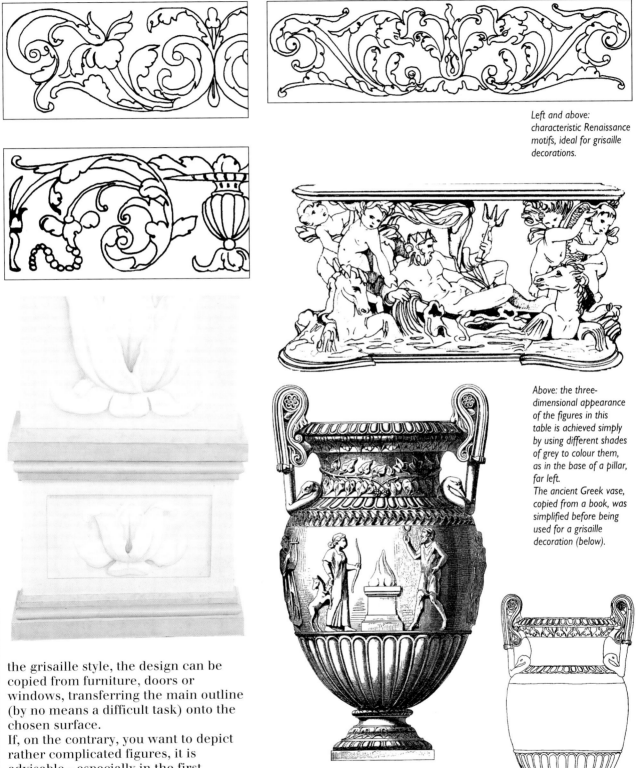

Left and above: characteristic Renaissance motifs, ideal for grisaille decorations.

Above: the three-dimensional appearance of the figures in this table is achieved simply by using different shades of grey to colour them, as in the base of a pillar, far left.
The ancient Greek vase, copied from a book, was simplified before being used for a grisaille decoration (below).

the grisaille style, the design can be copied from furniture, doors or windows, transferring the main outline (by no means a difficult task) onto the chosen surface.

If, on the contrary, you want to depict rather complicated figures, it is advisable - especially in the first instance - to purchase designs already marked with light and shade outlines in an art shop or one of the many text books in the field available from good bookshops. It will then suffice, once the design is transferred, to paint in the shaded areas copying the example.

WHAT'S NEEDED

Colours:
1-white, 2-black,
3-ochre, 4-blue
Colour A-white plus
black plus blue
Colour B-white plus
black plus ochre
Colour C-white plus
black
Colour D-colour C plus
black

Materials:
pencil, eraser, pencil-
sharpener, cutter,
paper tape, graphite
paper, ruler,
set-square, brushes,
bristle brush, 4, 6 and
8 mm retouching
brushes, 8 mm flat
brush, sponge

Screen with imitation Renaissance stuccos

The ideal base for grisaille decoration is a plain, dark colour, so that it highlights the overlying decoration, once the design is transferred and protected by masking.

1- Firstly, paint the main field of the decoration in a medium colour, a light beige similar to off-white (colour B); it should be rather diluted to avoid covering the lines of the drawing.

2- Having established the light source, use a 6 or 8 mm synthetic sable retouching brush to begin painting the shadow areas. Use a very diluted colour and moisten the surface with a sponge before applying the colour. Before the paint dries, work over it with a moist flat brush to blur the colour outwards so that a clear-cut line of colour is not produced.

3- When the paint is dry, use a synthetic sable retouching brush with a finer tip to intensify the colour of the most deeply shaded areas, starting with grey (colour C), which should be darkened with a little black (colour D); always moisten the surface in advance and "pull" the colour well.

4- When this is also dry, use the tip of a fine brush to apply small highlights of not very diluted absolute white in small areas where the light falls. Using colour C (as already used for the shaded areas), create the thrown shadows on the coloured base of the decoration using a flat brush.
Protect the work with two or three coats of matt water-based lacquer.

	1		2		3		4

1

2

4

Steps 1, 2, 3 & 4
show how the stucco
effect gradually increases
in depth.
Below: the finished
screen with Renaissance
motifs imitating stucco;
right: one of the
panels.

3

A   B   C   D

The Grotesque

Towards the middle of the 15th century, in the early Renaissance period, artists rejected Mediaeval art and took Roman and Greek art as their sole source of inspiration (Greek works were then only known through Roman copies).

Linear perspective emerged in the early Renaissance - the combination of rules which made it possible to reproduce a three-dimensional space on two-dimensional canvas or wall surfaces.

Subsequently, a less severe style was developed in which the rigour of geometry and perspective became less important in comparison with the taste for decoration and refined forms, typical of the courts of the period.

It was precisely against this background that the grotesque style emerged, a capricious and bizarre combination of fantastical plant forms and small human and animal figures painted on walls. The term used to define this kind of wall decoration originates from the "grottoes" of the Domus Aurea of Emperor Nero, where the paintings in this style can still be admired.

The decorations painted by Giovanni da Udine (1487-1564) on the ceilings and walls of the Vatican "Loggias" are a fine example of Renaissance grotesque.

Above: a grotesque mask painted on an imitation marble base.
Opposite: grotesque decorations on the walls of the boudoir of Marie Antoinette at Fontainebleau.

By the end of the 17th century, the style began to change becoming more delicate. Figures were painted as if they were floating weightlessly and the natural world, especially plant life, was studied in all its decorative possibilities. This saw the emergence of forms and figures with a more vertical extension and sinuous, almost flame-like forms.

Developments of this kind of decoration typified the Rococo period, which flourished especially in the period of Louis XV.

A typical example of this style is the ceiling of Kensington Palace, London, painted by William Kent and distinguished by continuous scrolling lines and precious colours, at times bright, at times delicately shaded.

Below and right: typical motifs of grotesque decoration.

Around the middle of the 18th century, excavations began in the city of Pompeii, bringing the buildings of the Roman city to light. The mural decorations were described in the treatise "Specimen of ancient decorations from Pompeii", published in London in 1825. Following these discoveries and the publications which spread knowledge of them, it became fashionable to decorate interiors with grotesque paintings inspired by the murals of Pompeii, a fashion which remained in vogue throughout the 19th century.

Painter-decorators are still inspired today by the wall decorations of previous centuries to recreate period atmospheres and settings.

Ancient techniques and colours

Grotesque decoration is repeated symmetrically on ceilings and walls but tends not to create the illusion of depth or space.

The decorative effect is based solely on colour matching and harmony of design. In the 17th century, neutral shades of grey, brown, umber, greenish, pinkish and reddish earths were generally used. Deeper blues, pea green and yellow date from the end of the 18th century. Only much later, with the introduction of chemical-based paints, was the range of colours employed significantly extended.

In ancient times, grotesque decorations were made using fresco and encaustic painting.

The first involves mixing pigments in water and applying to still fresh plasterwork. The pigments, however, undergo unwanted changes in colour caused by chemical reactions with the moist base; thus, many artists preferred to use the "secco" technique, in which the painting is made on dry plasterwork. Encaustic painting, on the other hand, defines the application to a dry surface of paints mixed with hot wax, which enhances the shade and achieves a very bright finish.

With the passing of the centuries, various methods were evolved to achieve better and more durable results. For example, grease was added to the pigments to neutralize the acidity of the lime which, with the passing of time, caused the pigments to decompose and consequently the work to deteriorate. Decorations made with the fresco technique require not only fine artistic skills and rapid execution (the decoration must be completed before the plasterwork dries) but also specific knowledge of how to apply the colours. Yet even beginners can produce effective imitations of the grotesque style using materials now available commercially and using 19th century techniques. Even today painter-decorators continue the tradition of antique frescoes to recreate the atmosphere and settings of times gone by.

THE GROTESQUE ON WOOD

Grotesque should not be viewed exclusively as a kind of mural decoration.
A composite wooden door frame or a simple wooden cornice can be adapted to this kind of decoration.
In this case, the modest dimensions of the task mean that water-paints can be used in place of earths. In any case, using significantly diluted water-paints in natural colours such as red oxide, umber, sienna and ochre, it is possible to achieve the characteristic

Above: a small wooden trunk decorated with marble inlays and a medallion depicting a grotesque mask.
Left: two stages in the grotesque decoration above a door.

natural effect of this form of decoration.

1- Apply two matt water-based base coats and glass-paper with paper n. 230. The surface does not have to be perfectly smooth.

2- Use graphite paper to transfer the design (adapted to the dimensions of the cornice).

3- To set off the decoration paint in a line around the design with red oxide darkened with the addition of black.

4- Using sable brushes of suitable sizes, colour in the grotesque painting with soft, diluted colours in two stages to obtain the shadows, lightening them with white before adding the highlights. Once the paint is dry, apply two coats of matt water-based protective compound and then the antiquating patina, with special emphasis on the outlines of the frame.

WHAT'S NEEDED

Colours:
1-white, 2-red oxide,
3-umber, 4-sienna,
5-ochre, 6-blue,
7-black

Materials:
glass-paper, graphite
paper, 4, 6 and 8 mm
sable retouching
brushes

1

2

3

| | 1 | | 2 | | 3 | | 4 | | 5 | | 6 | | 7 |

4

Very effective decorations can be achieved using classic grotesque designs enhanced with frames in contrasting colours.

THE GROTESQUE IN MURALS

Ideas and inspiration for grotesque decorations can be taken from art books and furnishing magazines. However, if you don't want to make your own grotesque design, it is possible to enlarge an example with a photocopier and then transfer it onto the surface.

Having selected the design it is a good idea to pause for reflection in front of the wall to be decorated and carefully observe the whole room because, unlike the majority of paintings, a mural decoration is directly influenced by the surrounding environment. It becomes an integral part of it. To ensure a good result, it may be necessary to simplify the design and slightly modify the colour shades, but this can only be established through careful observation of the entire setting.

Grotesque is repeated in insets on walls and/or ceilings. So, having selected the design to be reproduced, study the dimensions of the framing which will contain it to adapt it to the decoration.

The design selected for this grotesque painting was divided into squares to facilitate progress of work.

WHAT'S NEEDED

Colours:
1-yellow, 2-red,
3-umber,
4-natural sienna,
5-blue, 6-green,
7-burnt sienna

Materials:
stippling wire, spirit-level, paper tape, graphite paper, brushes, 4, 6 and 8 mm synthetic sable retouching brushes, acrylic glue

1- Having defined the size of the squares into which the grotesque decoration is to be divided, transfer these measurements onto the pre-prepared surface. Use the spirit-level to check the correctness of these markings. Use a soft-tipped pencil or stippling wire for marking out.

2- Apply the base colour to the squares. Usually, the shade used for the base on which the motifs of the cornice are drawn differs very little from that on which the grotesque decoration as such is made, but other colours can be used to harmonize everything with the overall setting.

| 1 | 2 | 3 | 4 | 5 | 6 | 7 |

1

2

Preparation of the base is done in two stages. First of all, apply the chosen colour (neutral shade) to the pre-prepared surface, having diluted it with a little water first to make it rather fluid. Before this coat dries, dab it with a sponge. In this example, beige was used (adding a little black, less umber and a dash of ochre to warm to a white water-paint).
When this is completely dry, sponge over with a diluted darker colour (umber) to give the surface an antiquated patina.
Sponging should be done very delicately and irregularly, always accompanying the underlying colour so that it takes on an "aged" appearance. Use a different colour to paint the base of the cornice, which again should be sponged with dilute umber.

3- Having prepared the base, transfer the grotesque design. The transfer operation is easy but some precautions are needed.
First and foremost, rub the copy paper with a cloth before attaching

3

4

it to the wall in order to remove the excess graphite which may otherwise soil the surface; don't forget to secure the drawing with tape so that it cannot move and complete the transfer with great care.
Be careful not to rest your arm on the paper and, having marked out a few lines, make sure that the drawing is still positioned correctly. Mistakes can be cancelled by wiping with a moist rag.

4- Once the drawing has been transferred, it can be painted.
It is best to use powder pigments (earths) dissolved in a 50% solution of water and acrylic glue. The pigments are called "earths" because, in the past, they were all natural products. Nowadays, they are synthetic chemical products sold in a wide range of colours. Earths make it possible to achieve delicate veil-like colouring which is well-suited to a period grotesque decoration. In this case, acrylic paints were used for the base of the decoration and earths diluted in water and acrylic glue for the figures.

HINTS AND TIPS

When preparing paint, make sure lumps do not form. If necessary, add a little more water but remember that this lightens the shade.
When the paint is ready try it out on the base to verify the effect. Remove this paint before it dries with a moist sponge.
If you want to intensify the col-our, add a little move pigment. If, on the other hand, you want to darken it add umber. Add water to increase transparency.

5

6

7

HINTS AND TIPS

When deciding on the size of the synthetic sable retouching brush to be used, bear in mind that it must enable you to work as quickly as possible.
Never saturate the brush with paint, since it could run over the rest of the decoration.
Paint calmly but quickly: brush strokes should be unhesitant as if working at speed on fresh plaster. Don't worry about minor mistakes or smudges: they actually enhance resemblance to ancient grotesque decorations.

5- Before starting the final stage, it is advisable to do a colour trial to make sure that everything is harmonious.
It is also advisable to make a small copy of the design and colour it as this will be a useful guide as decoration work progresses.

6- Once the paints are ready, you can begin to decorate. It is always a good idea to keep a sponge and a bucket of water handy as they are essential if mistakes have to be corrected. Always bear in mind that before resuming the task it is necessary to wait until the cancelled surface is completely dry.

7- When all the main fields have been painted, wait until they are completely dry before proceeding. Where darkening is required, apply the same colour with distinct brush strokes. To verify that the effect obtained is exactly as intended, take a few steps back from the decoration every now and then.

8- When the "colouring" stage is over stand back to check the overall effect. If no retouching is needed, the protective coating can be applied, as follows. Wipe the decoration with a moist cloth to remove every trace of

dust; then, using a new or thoroughly clean brush, apply the protective coating (use a commercial acrylic solution), having first diluted it with water following the instructions provided with the product. When this coat is dry, apply a second coat, "pulling" the compound well so that drops are not formed and making sure every part of the decoration is covered.
If you want to brighten the decoration, apply a little wax (solid white wax is available from ironmongers) and polish the whole surface with a soft, lint-free cloth. To speed up this task, it is advisable

To decide which areas to darken, study carefully the two photographs (right): chiaroscuro highlights the overall impression.

8

Decorative motifs can be used to set off the grotesque decoration.

9

10

to mix the wax with a little turpentine and then apply with a brush.

9- To antiquate the decoration even more, before applying the protective coating glass-paper certain areas lightly with paper n. 240-340; this will smear the colour a little, giving the decoration a more "worn" appearance.

To set off this effect, before applying the wax, dye it with a pinch of umber.
As far as the cornice is concerned, if you are in a hurry or if the grotesque decoration has been made on a piece of canvas or panelling so that it can be positioned later, finish it off with a stucco cornice decorated to imitate marble.

TROMPE L'OEIL

Translated literally, "trompe l'oeil" means "to trick the eye". Trompe l'oeil is thus a pictorial decoration which "tricks" the observer, even for just a few seconds, into thinking that the scene depicted is real and not a reproduction.

You can imitate a simple marble or wooden cladding on a wall or even a window through which a landscape can be seen. In this pictorial technique, it is very important to achieve a three-dimensional effect in the decoration, otherwise it will end up not being a visual illusion but merely a flat surface. To do this, you must recreate the exact perspectives of the scene and know how to use light and shade.

The first examples of trompe l'oeil date back to the Ancient Greeks and Romans. At Pompeii, we can still admire trompe l'oeil decorations of gardens or colonnades beyond which landscapes can be glimpsed; they were used to create the illusion of being a source of light in windowless rooms. Some of these decorations have very delicate colours which create the impression of distant gardens and undefined outlines which observers can "enter" by using their imagination.

The trompe l'oeil decorations of Ancient Rome were copied during the Middle Ages, especially in Italy, but the technique became most popular during the Renaissance period. Perspective and its rules made it possible to depict architectural forms and disappearing colonnades very faithfully, which could not previously be depicted in a realistic manner. During the Renaissance, even very famous artists were commissioned to decorate the palaces and residences of the nobility and for some considerable time the style of this kind of decoration was especially influenced by the taste of Italian painter-decorators. Only later, when the culture of France in the 17th century came to dominate the whole of Europe, bringing the Baroque with it, did trompe l'oeil decorations also make their appearance in the new style.

Opposite: a view of Piazza di Pietra, Rome. Above: an imitation window with books and a flowering plant in a vase on a windowsill.

A door becomes a bookcase, thus becoming completely "camouflaged" in the context of the room.
Left: the initial draft.
Right: the finished trompe l'oeil decoration.

This form of decoration was especially popular in the 18th century, along staircases and imposing corridors, on the ceilings of noble palaces and the houses of the gentry. Trompe l'oeil became the focal point in the decoration of rooms and taste returned again to neo-classic landscapes with colonnades and ruins. Since then, it has become ever more widely used, to the extent that today it is almost a commonplace. When making a trompe l'oeil decoration, it must be adapted to personal requirements - i.e. the surface and the place where it is to be made. The effect of trompe l'oeil decoration, in fact, depends less on the technique of execution than on the way it blends with its setting. Unlike a painting, a trompe

A roof terrace in Rome almost becomes a sitting room. The door to the store-room is camouflaged by a trompe l'oeil decoration reproducing the antique majolica decoration of the terrace.

A fresco copied from an art book almost becomes a "designer" decoration.

l'oeil decoration is chosen for a specific place and must therefore harmonize well with the existing setting.

Design and selection of the base surface

More than in any other decorative form, to make a trompe l'oeil decoration, it is essential to dedicate a great deal of time to planning the task.
This kind of technique can be carried out on walls, canvas or wood. Before painting the surface, it must be carefully prepared, as already explained.
It is obvious that the location and the size of the trompe l'oeil you want to paint are vital as regards the preparation of the base. A wall in poor condition or else lacquered and waxed will require a great deal of time and effort before it can be decorated; in this instance, it is preferable to use a wooden panel which can be affixed to the wall, if the draft is not very big, or even a canvas. This approach also makes it possible to move the decoration if so required. We have previously described how such surfaces can be prepared but, in the case of wood, it is worth pointing out that, since water-based products are used, it is best to use "maritime" wood, so-called because it was used in the interior finishing of ships.
This wood can even be cut to thicknesses of 4.5 mm ($^1/_4$ in) with the assurance that it will not warp.

Left: the walls of a study decorated with a "lambris" in imitation "lumachella carnacina" marble.
Below: the illusion of space created by a "open window" overlooking a country landscape.

Composite wood is also a suitable material. Preparation simply requires two or three coats of matt water-based protective compound (always apply the first coat to both sides of the panel) and light glass-papering with paper n. 180 or n. 200.

If you decide to paint a trompe l'oeil decoration on a terrace or portico outside, it is essential to use "maritime" wood treated with two coats of water-based base compound (products for acrylic paints also ensure water-proofing) on both sides of the panel and, especially, on the cut borders. If you intend to work directly on an outside wall you should first make sure that it is not affected by rising damp and coat it with an opaque base for acrylic paints.

Selecting the subject

The subject depends in the first instance on the size of the surface available for decoration, then on the setting and on the angle of observation.

You cannot decide to paint a window if there is not enough space to paint it life-size. In trompe l'oeil, unlike paintings, the foreground must be life-size, otherwise the "trick" simply will not work.

Smaller works of trompe l'oeil can be made with showcases, bookcases or niches containing small ornaments. The ideal surface for trompe l'oeil

should be rather large, preferably not interrupted by radiators, electricity plugs or switches, although there is always a way of camouflaging them in the decoration using the imitation marble technique, for instance, to harmonize the setting and make these irregularities less evident.

The setting of the decoration should also be carefully studied, since different subjects should be chosen for an office, a lounge, a bedroom or a dark corridor. Even the architecture of the setting plays an important role in the choice of subject, together with the style and dominant colours.

In a room with many windows, where it is by no means necessary to create an impression of the outdoors, it is hardly appropriate to paint a country landscape which would immediately seem out of

A surreal door opening out onto a dreamy swimming pool sets off a modern room.

place. If curtains and objects are to be included in the trompe l'oeil, it is a good idea to make them similar to those already present in the room. A door can be "hidden" by painting an imitation bookcase; in the same way, the shelves or niches in a wall can be made to seem symmetrical.

The angle of observation is extremely important in trompe l'oeil. If the wall is large but can be observed close up, it should have an excellent foreground and a very blurred background to create the illusion of space. A trompe l'oeil seen from a certain distance, on the other hand, may have less precise details since it is the overall view that matters.

Before starting the painting task every decorator, having selected and prepared the base, should pause for thought in front of the white wall to gather ideas and make sketches.

You can use your own imagination in trompe l'oeil, since the decoration does not necessarily have to reproduce a real view. In a modern house even an imaginary landscape can help to open out a wall and create a dream-like atmosphere.

Imitation marble: tiles and masking

One of the easiest trompe l'oeil decorations that can be made because the rules of perspective are not involved, is imitation marble, ideal for whole walls or to imitate architectural details such as columns, windowsills and windows themselves. For walls, it is best to use marbles having soft colours to avoid a sensation of heaviness, such as Sienna yellow and "lumachella carnacina".

As already mentioned in the chapter dealing with imitation marble, natural marbles are found in a great many varieties. When reproducing them on a wall, it is essential to copy the specific characteristics of the chosen marble, such as the colour shade and the vein pattern.

To decorate a very large surface in imitation marble, it should be divided into tiles. To achieve the most realistic decoration possible, these must always be of the same size as commercial products (approx. 60x80 cm/ 24x32 in). Larger tiles would be impossible to produce and transport and would immediately seem "fake", compromising the outcome of the decoration. The same can be said for décor, a pictorial imitation using colours different from those of natural marble would again be unrealistic.

Before designing the imitation marble tiles, measure the wall itself

To achieve a marble effect on large surfaces such as the walls of a room, it is best to opt for veined marbles with soft colours. Above: a wall decorated in Sienna yellow marble and left, a decoration in "lumachella carnacina".

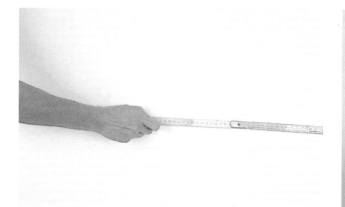

and then divide these dimensions by the size of standard marble tiles.

If the result is not a round number share out the remainder among the tiles or even juggle the standard dimensions in an effort to find a round number. In this case it is better to reduce the dimensions of standard tiles rather than increase them.

Having defined the upper limit, use a ruler to mark out a straight line perfectly parallel to the floor and then add the points which define the chosen format of the tiles. Now mark out the bottom edge; to be sure that the tile position marks on the top and bottom lines align, use a plumb-line.

To draw in the lines joining the marks on the wall use a ruler and pencil or, better still, a stippling wire (a receptacle filled with powder, ideally sienna earth, with a roll of wire inside. When the wire is stretched between the two points to be joined, it can be pinched gently between the fingers to

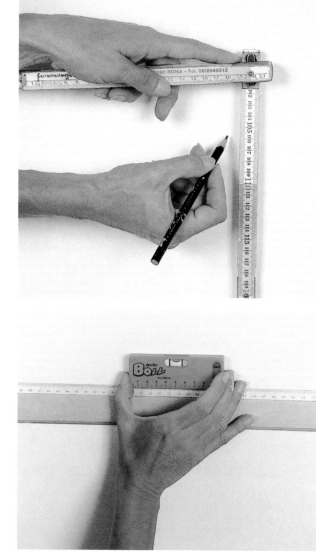

Above: having measured the wall, calculate the format of each tile and mark out (left). Below: trace out a line parallel to the floor using a spirit-level; add the joint lines starting from this reference line.

leave a faint mark on the wall).

The masks are then prepared. This requires considerable care. The tape must exactly follow the lines marked out beforehand and must also adhere to the wall perfectly to avoid paint getting underneath. The task can be speeded up by masking tiles in alternation, i.e. mask one, leave one free. Be very careful when positioning the tape because mistakes are easily made. It is best to mark out the tile to be painted first with a

pencil line. This is because having finished masking, a series of identical tape lines will be left and it will not always be easy to distinguish those which have already been prepared from the others.

Remove the tape from the tiles which have been painted and reposition it inside the tile to free the surface still to be painted. Always make the tape less sticky before using it by applying it first to a clean surface.

Above, from left: the tape masking sequence for the marble tiles, starting from the joint line marks (made using the stippling wire) between the top and bottom lines through to the positioning of the tape to mask the various tiles. The tape should always be made less sticky, even by applying it first to your trousers.

1

2

3

Imitation Sienna yellow marble

An imitation Sienna yellow marble decoration was chosen for a professional studio.

WHAT'S NEEDED

Colours:
1-white, 2-ochre, 3-black
Colour A-white plus ochre
Colour B-white plus black and a little ochre to warm

Materials:
stippling wire, calculator, paper tape, ruler, pencil, eraser, sponge, 4 and 8 mm synthetic sable retouching brushes, 40 and 50 mm bristle brushes

1- Having first marked out and masked the tiles of imitation marble on the wall, the base can be painted after having moistened the surface well with a sponge.
Using different brushes for each colour (prepare them in different plates), try to create and blend areas of different colouring.
Natural Sienna marble has a huge variety of shades so specific quantities for colours A and B are not required: simply add more white to obtain a lighter shade or more darker water-paint for the opposite effect.
It is important not to dilute the paints too much to avoid them sticking to the wall while painting.
Complete the decoration calmly, "pulling" the paint well

| | 1 | | 2 | | 3 | | A | | B |

4

5

to avoid forming drops. Try to alternate the colours as far as possible by blurring them together but make sure that the final colouring is not entirely uniform.

2- Having prepared the base of all the tiles, make sure they are all completely dry. Remove the tape between the tiles and then paint in the vein pattern. Before starting, it is advisable to prepare everything you will need for the task, especially the paints (white, ochre and colour B) so that they are within easy reach.

3- Using the synthetic sable retouching brushes (the size of the veins depends on the thickness of the brush), add the ochre in small, dilute quantities so that it is rather fluid and brushes easily onto the tile already painted. Always moisten the surface. The veins dry very quickly so, to speed up the task, it is advisable to finish one tile completely before moving onto the next. If you use only one brush, clean it thoroughly before using a different colour since the veins must have well-defined shades.

4- Continue with white and colour B, bearing in mind that the veins in Sienna yellow marble intersect and separate, widen and thin out to form bands in a single direction, interrupted every now and then by an isolated vein. The design possibilities are endless but it is important that the tiles do not all have the same vein patterning.

5- To highlight the interruptions of the vein pattern and create the impression that they really are set into genuine marble, cut off certain veins suddenly on the lines separating the different tiles. Having completed the task and if the result is satisfactory, apply two coats of shiny or matt water-based protective compound.

Then soften the wax, heating it slightly or adding half a teaspoon of turpentine, and apply it with a brush to the dry lacquer.

Top: cornices in imitation wood enclosing a landscape and other objects.
Right: this cornice in imitation marble has a frame with light and shade effects to achieve a three-dimensional appearance.

Three-dimensional appearance: drafting and the rules of linear perspective

When making a trompe l'oeil in which not only are materials such as marble or wood to be imitated but a three-dimensional appearance of various objects is also required, such as the cornices of imitation marble or wooden frames, choose your frame design and then apply light and shade as already described in the chapter dealing with grisaille. Prepare the cornice in imitation marble and, having designed the frame free-hand or with graphite paper, use a very dilute, greyish colour to create the veiled shading and denser white to create the highlights.

The same technique is used to reproduce wooden frames with carvings.

To interpret a three-dimensional space a scale draft must be prepared so that perspective can be laid out.

Having selected the kind of subject and found a source of inspiration (landscape photographs, objects, plants, animals, cornices or architectural structure-work, arches or columns), decide on

the angle of observation and then rough out the draft which is simply a scale representation of the scene to be painted on the wall.

Architectural motifs for a column indicating the proportions of the elements. Right: examples of different kinds of arch.

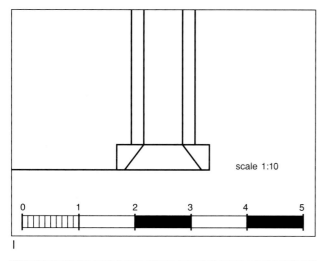

scale 1:10

0   1   2   3   4   5

1

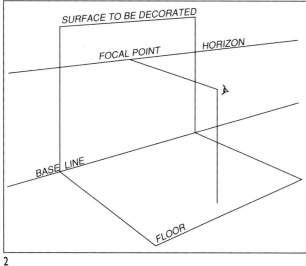

SURFACE TO BE DECORATED

FOCAL POINT   HORIZON

BASE LINE

FLOOR

2

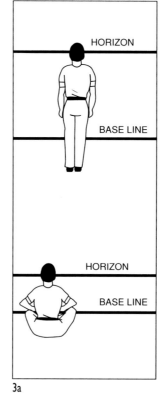

HORIZON

BASE LINE

HORIZON

BASE LINE

3a

1- Firstly, select the scale, by deciding how many cm (in) of graph paper correspond to a meter (ft) on the wall. For example, if 1 cm (¹/₂ in) of the draft sheet represents 10 cm (4 in) of wall, then the scale is 1:10.

2- Prepare a scale drawing of the dimensions and outline of the surface to be decorated, then mark out the "base line" which, if the surface to be painted covers the entire wall or reaches down to the floor, will coincide with the base of the surface just drawn.

3 & 3a - If the trompe l'oeil is to be painted on half a wall, such as a window about 1 m (³/₄ ft) from the floor, the lower edge should be drawn 10 cm (4 in)

from the base of the surface ("base line"). Having established the base line, now mark out the "horizon" as far from the base line as the viewpoint of the hypothetical observer: it is customary to calculate a distance of about 155 cm (61 in) from the base line (about 15 cm (6 in) in 1:10 scale); if the viewpoint is changed (for example, a trompe l'oeil which is only viewed when seated), the distance between the base line and the horizon also changes. The viewpoint is then defined on the horizon, i.e. the focal point, calculated by imagining a direct, perpendicular line between the observer's eyes and the decoration. Consequently on the scale drawing the viewpoint will be central if it is assumed that the observer stands in front of the centre of the decoration, or more to the right or left if the observer views the decoration from the right or left. It is essential to learn these steps in order to apply the rules of linear perspective. It was already mentioned above that it is possible to represent a three-dimensional scene on a flat surface (thus two-dimensional) using not only effects of light and shade (such as grisaille) but also the rules of perspective.

FOCAL POINT   HORIZON

START-POINT FOR THE TROMPE L'OEIL

START-POINT FOR THE TROMPE L'OEIL

BASE LINE

FLOOR

3

4

4a

4- Think of railway tracks: if we stand in the middle between them, although we know perfectly well that they are parallel, they seem to get closer together in the distance.

4a & 4b- If we equally think of rows of trees of the same height or a colonnade, the last tree or the last column, i.e. those furthest away from us, will seem smaller than those nearest to us.
As a result, we form a mental picture which in some way distorts reality: the tracks are really parallel and the columns are really all of the same height. This distortion occurs only if the tracks or trees extend into the distance, i.e. they seem to be moving away from us.
If, on the contrary, we observe a series of columns from the front or tracks from above, the columns all seem to be of the same height and the tracks are parallel. In the first case, the tracks and the imaginary line joining the height of the columns are called lines of perspective, i.e. lines of depth, since they tend to move towards the horizon and, visually speaking, appear to get closer together. In the second case, the tracks and the line joining the height of the columns run parallel to the horizon and do not undergo visual modification.

Top: railway tracks disappearing into the distance and the different heights of a row of trees.
Below: the columns in a small parapet parallel to the horizon all appear to be of the same height.

4b

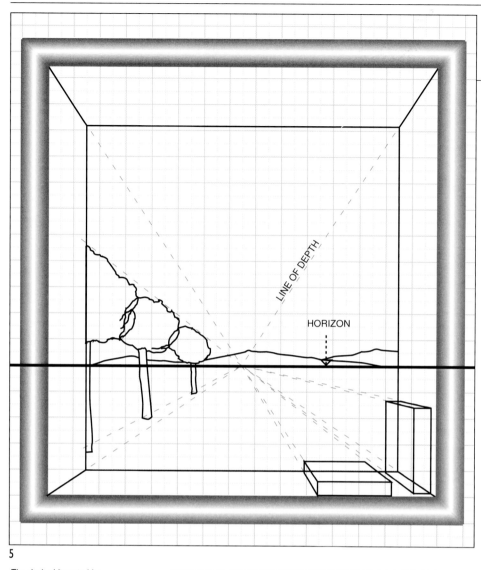

5

The dashed lines in blue represent lines of perspective; the vertical and horizontal lines of the books, parallel or vertical to the horizon, are not lines of perspective and thus do not change.

LINE OF DEPTH

HORIZON

5- To depict these distortions on a sheet of paper you only have to apply the simple rules of linear perspective.
• Non-parallel straight horizontal lines on the horizon tend to converge at the focal point.
• Parallel horizontal lines on the horizon remain parallel.
• Vertical straight lines on the horizon remain so.
The figure shows how the lines of a row of shelves, a row of trees and the pages or a book are lines of perspective, since they are straight and not parallel on the horizon and they should be drawn as lines converging on the focal point; since the lines of the frame and the edges of the books are parallel and vertical to the horizon, they are not modified. These simple rules make it possible to

6

HORIZON
FOCAL POINT

155 cm
(61 in)

SCALE 1:10

10 cm
(4 in)

BASE LINE

HORIZON
FOCAL POINT

155 cm
(61 in)

SCALE 1:10

10 cm
(4 in)

BASE LINE

*Examples on
scaled paper
of reproductions
of the surfaces
to be decorated.*

7

draw objects and architecture viewed frontally; for more complicated designs, the topic requires more complete understanding.

6- It is worth pointing out that perspective can only be applied to outlines similar to geometrical figures such as cubes, squares or rectangles, etc.; mountains, trees, flowers and hills do not require such strict rules.

7- To give a better idea of depth in a landscape, colour shades can be modified to define details differently: hills,

plants and flowers will seem to be more distant if they become smaller, have lighter colours and less definite outlines. Objects in the foreground should therefore be sharp and the background gradually more blurred.

8- To achieve this effect, prepare not only a scale drawing but also a coloured version so that you can be sure about the final appearance of the decoration. Enlarge the scale draft on a photocopier and colour in with water-paints.

8

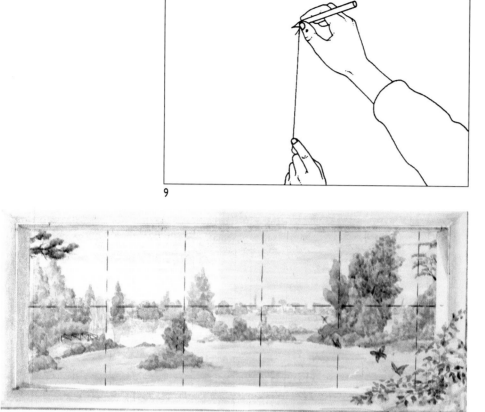

9

10

"squaring" technique in which the squares are drawn on the draft and transferred to size onto the wall; in this way, the decoration is divided into smaller sections which are easier to complete. Once the basic structure of the trompe l'oeil has been marked out, the smaller details and decorative elements can be inserted. Before drawing them in, refer to the colour draft to decide the parts to be painted immediately and those which can be painted subsequently. For example a distant tree can even be painted after having finished the sky; the frame around imitation marble can be finished off after the imitation marble itself is complete and inlays or a darker object can be added once the main field is ready.

Having prepared the draft of the trompe l'oeil and the surface to be decorated, work can begin. The design can be transferred onto the wall in several ways, which can be used together or alternately as required.

WHAT'S NEEDED

Materials:
hard pencil, pencil-sharpener, eraser, ruler, set-square, stippling wire, graphite paper, copy paper, string, projector, toothed roller for perforated patterns, sienna powder

9- Firstly, mark the focal point on the wall and then use a hard pencil and a ruler to mark out the main points of reference, i.e. the dimensions and the basic outline of the trompe l'oeil, such as the cornice surrounding it, the depth of a row of shelves and the height of a wall, etc. Having defined these points, slightly emphasize the lines with the stippling wire: if semi-circles, arcs or circles have to be drawn, use a pencil tied to a piece of string like a compass (someone else should hold the string steady in the centre of the circumference to be

marked out). Then keeping the string taut pull it around the fixed point and mark out the arc with the pencil. Touch up the markings by hand if necessary. Always referring to the draft for measurements, continue transferring the design, making sure from time to time that the lines of perspective effectively converge on the focal point. Mistakes in measurements are easily made. A length of string can be used in place of a ruler for rather large trompe l'oeil decorations.

10- The scene can be transferred onto the wall using the

11- All the elements which must be painted in light colours or in contrast with the base colour must be completed first, for example, the books in a bookcase or shells standing on a parapet in "pietra serena" etc. Friezes, vases and porcelain can be transferred onto the surface using graphite paper.
A repetitive element, such as small columns in a parapet can be copied onto copy paper and inserted as many times as needed using graphite paper.

12- At one time, repetitive elements were drawn in using the perforated pattern

11

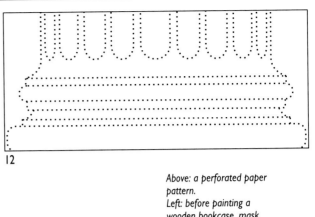

12

Above: a perforated paper pattern.
Left: before painting a wooden bookcase, mask the areas where objects will later be inserted.
Below: objects can easily be painted on top of a wall niche.

technique, which is still used today by many decorators. The design is made on rather stiff paper - copy paper is ideal - and then the outlines of the drawing are cut out (today, a special toothed roller is used, in the past, individual holes were made). The perforated pattern is then placed where the design is to be repeated and a pad dipped in sienna is dabbed over it. The powder passes through the holes, leaving clearly visible marks which can be enhanced free-hand. Perforated patterns can be kept and the design repeated endlessly. Today, the task can be speeded up using a projector so that the outlines can be copied very quickly. A projector and a colour draft can also be used to check the final effect of the trompe l'oeil.

ILLUSIONS OF INTERIORS

In rooms with large windows, walls separating communicating rooms and small surfaces, it is preferable to make a trompe l'oeil depicting a bookcase or shelves with ornaments rather than an imitation window.

When developing a trompe l'oeil depicting an interior, a great deal of time must be devoted to planning, since everything will be in the foreground. The objects to include in the scene must also be chosen with great care to ensure a harmonious result, as if selecting real objects to be placed in a real bookcase or showcase.

To design these imitation ornaments, it is a good idea to find photographs or drawings for inspiration.

For a bookcase, imagination can be used not only in the design of the frames and shelves but even in the objects and books to be included.

Opposite: an antique showcase with apothecary vases enclosed by wire netting.
This page: highly detailed objects which can be placed in imitation bookcases or on shelves.

1- Firstly, prepare a draft; if the trompe l'oeil is intended to reach down to the floor it is best to depict a cupboard instead of shelves, because the perspective of an object observed from above tends to become very distorted in relation to the distance of observation.

This is not the place to provide a highly detailed analysis of the rules of perspective which make it possible to paint a scene in relation to its distance from the observer; it is therefore assumed in a draft of a set of shelves that the depth of a 30 cm (12 in) shelf standing about 1 m (3 ¼ ft) from the floor will be 9-12 cm (3 ½ - 5 in) in dimension within the drawing. The same draft, excluding the shelves, can also be used for the exterior structure of a window without fittings.

Top: examples of colour drafts.
Right: example of how to develop a draft following the rules of perspective.

FOCAL POINT: 155 cm (61 in)
SHELF THICKNESS: 3 cm (1 ¼ in)
DISTANCE BETWEEN SHELVES: 26 cm (10 ¼ in)
DISTANCE FROM THE OBJECT: 12 cm (5 in)
HEIGHT FROM FLOOR: 105 cm (41 ¼ in)

103 x 130 cm (41 x 51 in)

HEIGHT OF OBJECT FROM FLOOR: 93 cm (37 in)

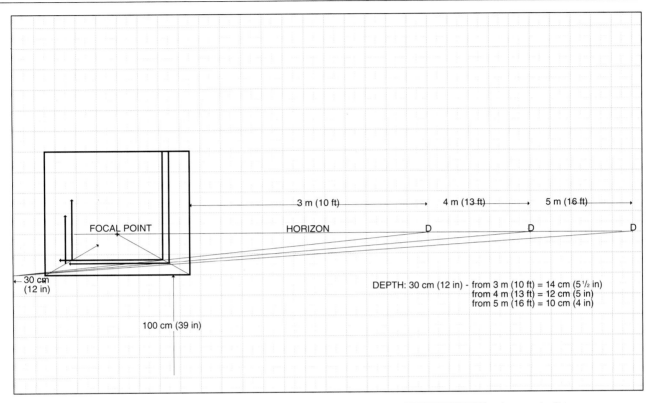

FOCAL POINT

3 m (10 ft)   4 m (13 ft)   5 m (16 ft)

HORIZON   D   D   D

30 cm
(12 in)

DEPTH: 30 cm (12 in) - from 3 m (10 ft) = 14 cm (5 ½ in)
from 4 m (13 ft) = 12 cm (5 in)
from 5 m (16 ft) = 10 cm (4 in)

100 cm (39 in)

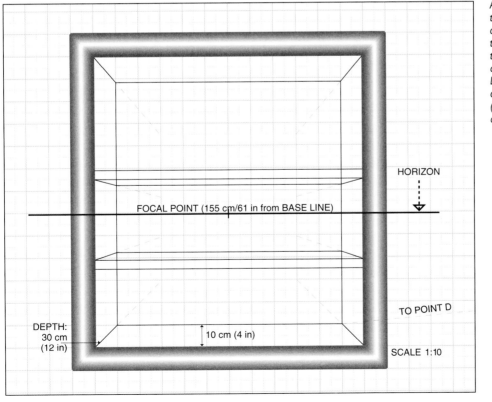

HORIZON

FOCAL POINT (155 cm/61 in from BASE LINE)

TO POINT D

DEPTH:
30 cm
(12 in)

10 cm (4 in)

SCALE 1:10

*An example of how
the distance between the
observer (D) and
the object determines
the variation in depth of
a shelf.
Left: the draft of a set
of shelves with 30 cm
(12 in) shelving seen from
a distance of 3 m (10 ft).*

2

2

3

3 3

3

2- Having designed the shelves and painted in the main structure of the trompe l'oeil, the individual decorative elements can now be painted, having first outlined and masked them.

3- The next step involves outlining and then painting the shadows thrown by each object, otherwise they would seem as though they are suspended in space. To paint in thrown shadows, use a very dilute paint, mixing a little black and umber with a small amount of the base colour. Before painting in these shadows, remember to moisten the surface (follow the technique indicated for grisaille). Maintaining the direction of the light source selected for the thrown shadows of each object, use a pencil to outline them. Once again, inspiration can be taken from reference photographs since they considerably simplify the study of shadow forms. Careful and minute observation of reality and trials will enable even beginners to mark out "realistic" shadow effects.

Left: an imitation showcase with different kinds of teapot. Bottom: an enlargement of one teapot.

Porcelain

If you don't want to attempt very complicated tasks of perspective but you have a steady hand and good copies of drawings or photographs of antique porcelain or old apothecary vases, then producing an effective trompe l'oeil is not difficult.

1- Having outlined the basic showcase, apply a coat of slightly bluish white (similar to the colour of porcelain) over the base. Use graphite paper to transfer the design of the teapots, making sure that they are seen from different heights because they will be placed on different shelves. The décor of the teapots themselves must be transferred very carefully to avoid soiling them with the graphite paper. Then mask out with paper tape and paint in the frame and interior of the showcase. Modify the colour in relation to the different kind of illumination of the base and the shelves.

2- Using a rather dilute colour, begin to paint in the teapots using retouching brushes of different sizes as required.

3- Prepare a very dilute shadow colour with black and blue and begin painting the shadow effects of each individual teapot, always following the

direction of light
illuminating the main
side fields of the
showcase.
Draw in the thrown
shadows and paint
them in on the base
with the same shade of
paint.

2

2

3

Having completed the showcase with all the teapots, the thrown shadows are painted in, achieving a much more realistic effect (below). Right: the showcase without shadowing effects is rather flat.

Books

As already mentioned, if the background of the bookcase is light or almost white, the objects can be painted in at a later stage having filled in the colouring of the main field. If the bookcase is in imitation wood or a colour other than white, the objects should be painted in and masked with paper tape before applying the base colour.

1- Books should be drawn life-size with a hard pencil and a ruler, starting from the spines. Then mark out the upper lines of perspective of the pages and the perpendicular line to the focal point at the back of the shelves, together with the lines of perspective of the bottom edge to determine the length of the upper lines.

2- Decoration of the books is a meticulous task requiring a steady hand and attention to detail.
First of all, mask the books and then prepare the paints (which should be diluted) attempting to achieve a good match. Beginning with the spine, moisten the surface before applying the paint with regular, decisive strokes. Using a clean and moist 10 or 12 mm bristle brush, "pull" the colour towards the centre before it dries to reproduce the roundness of the spine. Clearly, books in alternating positions can be painted simultaneously.

3- Having completed the main field, intensify the roundness of the spine using a darker but rather diluted colour. With a retouching brush, paint in the titles and the label decorations. To finish, intensify the gaps between the books with umber and a retouching brush.

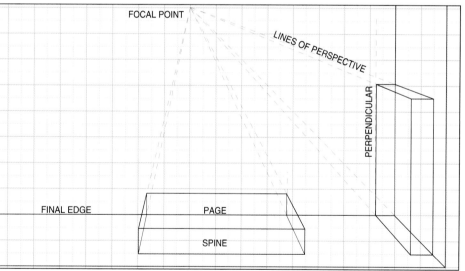

FOCAL POINT

LINES OF PERSPECTIVE

PERPENDICULAR

FINAL EDGE　　　PAGE

SPINE

1

2

3

ILLUSIONS OF EXTERIORS

Trompe l'oeil decorations imitating exteriors inside rooms are generally rather large. It is a good idea to organize the room by protecting the surrounding floor and furniture with sheets of plastic or newspapers and setting up a work table near the surface to be decorated and, in the case of a rather high trompe l'oeil, steps or a trestle on which the materials required can be placed.

1- When painting a landscape trompe l'oeil, the actual painting - once the design has been transferred - should proceed from the background towards the foreground. Observe the scene as if it were made up of several levels, each at a different distance from anyone looking at it. There should be at least four planes or levels in every trompe l'oeil decoration.

WHAT'S NEEDED

Materials:
bristle and ox bristle brushes of various sizes, synthetic sable retouching brushes of various sizes, flat-tipped brushes, sponge, steel wool, water-paints, earths, acrylic glue, paper tape, photographs or models for trompe l'oeil decoration

1

2- As can be seen in our examples, the foreground generally involves an object on a windowsill. Here again, the object should be chosen not only in relation to the overall harmony of the composition but also to the pictorial skills of the decorator.
A sensation of distance can be enhanced not only through perspective but also different use of colours and pictorial precision between one plane and another.
Progressing by levels then presents less risk of painting a decorative element belonging to a different plane too precisely in colours which are too strong. Moreover, by beginning from the last level, i.e. the one nearest the horizon, there is less risk of making mistakes, since the colours and precision of the

2

If you want to paint sky, bear in mind that the colours must be pale and diluted. Three progressively darker colours are needed (the sky on the horizon is always lighter).

1- Use paper tape to mask the parts which are not to be painted and begin to paint the sky.
Always moisten the painting can be slightly accentuated as you move down through the different levels.

3- For the foreground shadows, use colours of different luminosity to distinguish a shadow area from an illuminated area. Where it is impossible to diversify colouring in relation to illumination from the outset (as in the case of an imitation marble vase or a gypsum statue) use umber. Also paint in the thrown shadow on the parapet. For the shadow effects involving more distant objects, use colours of different intensity in the shaded and illuminated areas from the start.

Top: a photograph used for reference is indispensable when painting shadow effects.

3

surface before applying the paint so that it dries less rapidly and to make shading easier. Brushes must be clean and moist. Pass over the areas where different shades meet repeatedly to blend the colours.

2- If clouds are to be painted once the sky is dry, blur the colour in two or three places with the sponge and brush, applying two or three shades of white. This helps give volume to the clouds. Always moisten the surface before painting.

1

2

1

2

Plants and flowers

Having painted the sky and the distant landscape, the trees and hills in the intermediate level can be inserted before painting those in the foreground. Prepare a palette of colours, mixing them only as used to obtain different shades of green.

1- To paint very dense foliage prepare a base in an intermediate colour which reflects the green shading of the plant (a photograph or sample are always useful), then use a flat bristle brush to apply short brush strokes.

2- Use a much darker colour to intensify the shade in certain places to create shadow areas and then a much lighter colour for highlights.

3

If a plant with more open foliage is being painted use a smaller brush and tiny brush strokes, so that the sky remains visible between the leaves.

3- For complete trees use a dark and a light colour to achieve a more rounded appearance.
Use this approach also when painting bushes. Apply little touches of a darker colour to the base colour to create shaded areas and shape the plant and a lighter shade for highlights.

4

4- To paint climbing plants almost in the foreground use strong brush strokes and dark green to paint the main foliage. Take care not to smudge the groups of flowers painted beforehand should you decide not to mask them. Then use a lighter shade to paint the leaves more in the foreground, without giving too much emphasis to the veins. Afterwards, paint in the other flowers.

5- If the climbing plant should appear to be more distant, use the same technique but be careful not to emphasize the colours. The flowers should appear like little dots in a variety of shades.

6- To paint flowers and leaves in the foreground, several shades of paint should be used. To paint a rose use a synthetic sable brush of suitable size and prepare an intermediate colour, a much darker colour for the shaded areas and a much lighter colour for the highlights. Blend the colours together in order to disguise the brush strokes.
If a bunch of flowers of the same colour is to be painted, it is advisable to distinguish the colour of each flower and the precision of the details in order to emphasize the three-dimensional appearance of the composition.

7- In the same way it is best when painting a green plant not to devote the same attention to detail for

5

7

all the leaves. The
leaves to the rear, or
those in shade, should
be darker and less
detailed.

6

175

The sea

Since the sea has an enormous range of colours, trompe l'oeil decorations depicting seaside scenes are extremely effective, especially if inserted into an appropriate setting.

1- If a distant landscape is being painted, the technique is the same as that already described for the sky. Always moisten the surface before painting so that the shades can be easily blurred together.
Chose the colour shades in relation to the scene to be painted (it is always a good idea to have a photograph to hand for reference).

2- The technique for seascapes nearer to the foreground is different. Simply wait until the paint is dry and then, using a brush of suitable size and a very light, almost white colour, paint in an intricate network of intersecting lines to imitate reflections.

3 & 3a- To paint an imitation swimming pool, prepare two shades of the same colour and apply the diluted lighter colour uniformly to the moistened surface. Once this is dry, use the slightly darker and again diluted colour to paint in the darker shades similar to irregular spots (3a). Wait until the paint is dry and then touch up in certain points to create the impression of depth. Lighten the

first colour even further by adding white and, when it is dense, add highlights inside the brighter areas.

4- Use darker colours for lakes and rivers bearing in mind the greenish reflections of vegetation and the shadows along the banks. The task is more pictorial than technical and requires the use of a wider range of colours if the scene is nearer to the foreground. If the lake or river is in the distance, the technique is the same as that described for the sea.

2

3

3a

4

Curtains

If the trompe l'oeil includes curtains, they must be designed in great detail, fold by fold.

1- If you want to paint a veil, apply a very dilute colour so that the outline is visible. Then pass over two or three times to round out the folds using a smaller synthetic sable brush.

2- Paint more deeply between the folds to accentuate the shadows and depth. If necessary a lighter colour than that of the base can be used to give highlights and accentuate roundness.

3- If the curtain is in heavier fabric, having painted in the outline, paint the main field following the folds and motifs of the fabric. Use paper if necessary to ensure that the edges between one colour and another are sharp, as in the case of stripes.

4- Then prepare a shadow colour. It is always a good idea to perform a trial before using it.

5- Using a synthetic sable brush of suitable size, paint in the shadows to give roundness and depth to the folds, passing over the areas you want to emphasize more than once. Use a much lighter colour for the highlights.

6 & 6a- The same technique can be used to give thickness and softness to a ribbon.

1

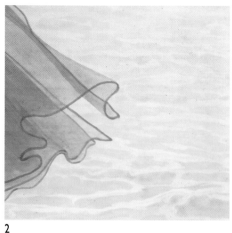

2

3

4

Having painted the main field, use two different shades to accentuate the twists of the ribbon and a shading colour to intensify the folds and the colour of the parts in shadow.

5

The folds of the curtain become extremely realistic thanks to the use of light and shade.

6

6a

Animals

Insects and butterflies are very common in gardens and can be great fun to paint. If the trompe l'oeil is intended to achieve the illusion of an imaginary scene, including familiar animals can enhance the illusion. Even if we think we can paint a dog or a cat from memory since they are common images, it is always a good idea to have a photograph to copy the shades of the coat and the expression of the muzzle.

To paint small animals you need a very thin brush and a steady hand. It will be very difficult to reproduce the coat well with acrylic paints, since they dry immediately and the painting task has to be completed very quickly.

1- Begin by drawing the outline of the animal, or transferring it with graphite paper, and then apply the base colour (using a lighter shade such a pinkish or greyish beige).

2- Now paint the muzzle, the folds of the body and, if present, the stripes and markings of its coat. If these are of different colours prepare two shades for each colour. Dab a flogger brush with very hard bristles many times against the palm of the hand to open the bristles and dip it into the colour for the deeper coat, remove the excess and dab slightly in the direction of the coat (copying the photograph or drawing used for reference). With another brush dipped into a lighter or darker colour as required, paint in the stripes so that they overlap the previous design and continue in this way, alternating the two colours. This will

The lizard and cricket in the trompe l'oeil shown here were inspired by a nature book.

1

2

3

create the impression of thick fur.
Using a dilute shadow colour, intensify the roundness of the animal and add shading; use a retouchng brush and a very light colour to paint the highlights.

3- If the coat of fur has several different shades, once the stripes have been painted in the two basic colours, use a 2 or 3 mm sable brush to apply the other colours in the same way.
Lastly, use a very light colour to paint the highlighted tips of fur. Having by now created the impression of fur use a dilute colour to paint in the shading and emphasize the outline of the muzzle.

3

3

3

GILDING AND SILVERING

Gilding involves the application of gold leaf or gold powder to any surface and has been widely used since ancient times for decorative purposes, alongside solid gold.

Gilt objects have been found dating back 3000 years, such as the mask of Tutankhamen, Pharaoh of the 18th Egyptian dynasty.

In more recent times, lower costs have encouraged the spread of gold leaf gilt work to decorate stuccos and architecture in churches and royal palaces. Currently, the technique is mainly used to enhance expensive picture frames or add a finishing touch to special decorations. Good gilding requires a great deal of experience and knowledge of specialist techniques such as the use of Bologna gypsum or bolus. However, very impressive decorations with low-cost materials can be achieved with gold-coloured metal leaf. As it is much heavier than pure gold leaf, it is easier to work and obviously much less expensive. If properly antiquated, excellent results can be achieved.

In this case, simply apply the sized and dressed gilt working techniques in simplified form. For silver work, bear in mind that silver is generally not used in its pure form but in different alloys with gold, zinc, copper, aluminium and so forth. It is one of the oldest known metals and, in the past, was often used for imitation gilding, since it was more economic than gilt and the silvered object, treated with several coats of gum lacquer, acquired the warm yellow colour of gold.

Above: a stucco picture frame has been gilded to adapt it to a period painting.
Opposite: an antique wooden frame was gilded again with metal leaf to imitate gilding.

GILDING

Gilding requires a range of materials which can only be found in good fine art shops.

Preparing the base

The surface to be gilded must be smooth and clean.
If gold leaf is used then the base should be prepared with several coats of Bologna gypsum mixed with rabbit skin glue.
For gilding using imitation gold leaf, apply three coats of sealing primer. When the base is dry, glass-paper well, the first time with paper n. 230 and then with paper n. 600, then clean the

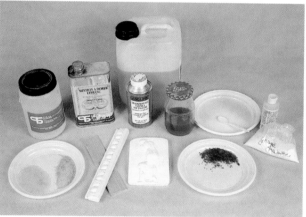

Top and above: the materials needed for gilding.
Bottom: Armenian bolus used to produce very shiny surfaces.

surface with a moist sponge. To imitate the colour of Armenian bolus, used in the gilding of Orthodox churches, apply a coat of acrylic red oxide, which can be mixed with a little ochre, yellow and white if a lighter shade is required, or umber for a more intense colour. Leave to dry and, if necessary, glass-paper quickly to eliminate any imperfections. Armenian bolus is a reddish, very greasy clay and, if mixed with rabbit skin glue, produces very shiny surfaces to which gold leaf adheres without the slightest risk of cracking. When using gold leaf, work in a dust-free, draught-free room so that the gold leaf cannot be blown away or split because of dust during the burnishing operation. To gild gypsum or earthenware objects, prepare the base as already described. Then apply the coat of red. It is advisable to use an ox bristle brush because it is soft and does not leave brush marks.
The glue can now be applied. There are two ways of applying glue: sizing and dressing.

Sizing: sizes are very special varnishes. Almost all grease-based or synthetic varnishes can be used to size a surface but, to ensure the inalterability of the metal leaf, they should be perfectly neutral and free of sulphur. Ready-to-use products are available commercially, complete with indications of

1　2　3　4

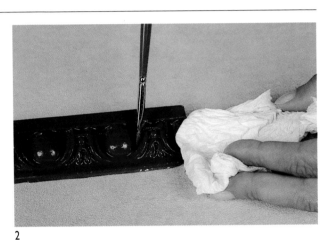

1

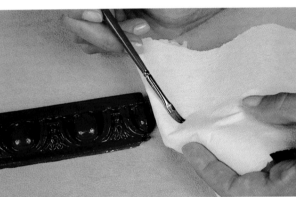

2

3

the time to wait between applying the coat of size and applying the metal leaf (15 minutes, 3 hours, 12 hours and more). The sizes which dry in 15 minutes are vinyl or acrylic products and should be diluted with water; the others, which are oily, are diluted with turpentine. This is important information since, if you want to accelerate drying times, the varnishes can simply be diluted.

1- To apply this kind of varnish, use an ox bristle brush with bristles which are not too short; begin from the top and apply the varnish uniformly over the entire surface.

2- If too much varnish is applied in crevices and deeper parts, it can be removed using a clean brush.

3- Remove excess product from the brush every now and then with a paper towel. Leave to dry in a dust-free, dry and well-aired (but not ventilated) place. The size is ready when it "crackles" slightly when barely touched with a finger. At this stage, the varnish is neither too moist nor too dry but is just sticky enough to ensure that the leaf adheres well to the base.

Dressing. In this case, the dressing has the same kind of function as the size. Dressings, in general are all those water-based substances (gum arabic) which, unlike size, swell and dissolve every time they are wetted, even if they are already dry. It is therefore relatively easy to remove gilding made in this manner simply by rubbing the surface with a moist sponge.
Sizing is therefore more durable than dressing but the latter is extremely useful for minor touching up jobs, small decorations, to gild paper or parchment or when not much time is available or if size is not ready to hand. In any case, having suitably protected the object (see finishing), the dressing will be reasonably durable. There are many different dressings but in this instance only some of the more simple agents should be taken into consideration bearing especially in mind the ease with which such

materials can be purchased. However, they should always be prepared as needed since they only keep for two or three days at most in a refrigerator.

Rabbit skin glue dressing. Swell the granules of rabbit skin glue overnight in water (1:10). When they are gel-like in appearance, dissolve using a bain marie without boiling. The solution must be kept lukewarm throughout the application procedure, otherwise it gels.

Gum arabic dressing. Available commercially ready-to-use or prepared by dissolving powdered gum arabic in water by means of a bain marie (1:3 or 1:4). Can also be worked cold because it doesn't harden.

Gum lacquer dressing. This substance does not dissolve in water. It can be purchased ready-to-use or in flakes which must be dissolved in 95° alcohol (1:10). It can be stored for some considerable time if sealed tightly in a can.

4

5

Dressed gilding is a rather fast procedure but equally one which requires a certain degree of skill if good results are to be achieved.

Beginning as ever from the top, apply the dressing with an ox bristle brush which is not dipped in too much product to avoid dripping. Since these substances dry very quickly proceed by sections. Interrupt the dressing task every now and then to apply the gold leaf.

It is advisable to alternate these sections leaving empty spaces which will be filled in later, so that the next application of dressing does not affect the gold leaf just applied before the dressing has had time to act.

Applying gold leaf

The gold leaf can now be applied to the prepared surfaces.

Imitation gilding. Imitation gilding is an alloy for the most part comprising copper with other metals, such as zinc and tin. It is available commercially in large sheets of a more or less intense colour of pure gold. However, the colour tends to change because of oxidation resulting from exposure to air. These sheets are much stronger and thicker than gold or silver leaf, so that they are less likely to break or crease. Because they are less expensive, they are ideal for beginners.

4- Delicately pick up the leaf with clean dry hands and place it on the cushion for cutting. If the object to be gilded has many reliefs or crevices it is best to cut the sheet into small pieces with a goldsmith's knife so that they adapt better to these shapes; even for flat surfaces, it is best not to use pieces which are rather large.

5- When the base surface is sized and the leaf applied as tautly as possible, press it down delicately with a flat ox bristle brush so that it adheres perfectly. When the entire surface has been coated, brush down with a bristle brush to remove any metal particles (which can be used to touch up gaps). To finish the task off still further, work over it, applying a certain pressure, with an ox bristle brush to that the leaf is "stretched". This eliminates "crinkles" and imperfections. If the base surface is dressed, do not touch the leaf once it is applied because it may break or move very easily.

Blow over the surface and immediately afterwards pass over with an ox bristle brush to facilitate adhesion to the base. If defects are seen, they can be remedied by repeating the operation.

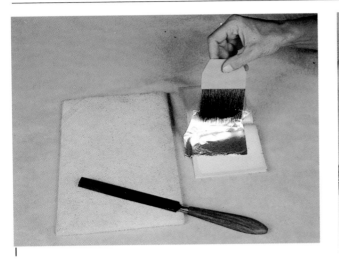

SILVERING

Silvering techniques, as far as sizing or dressing of the base surface are concerned, are carried out in the same way as gilding.
However, a number of special expedients are needed when applying silver leaf.

1- Silver leaf is sold commercially in small sheets. Like gold, it is a very ductile metal and can therefore be rolled into very thin sheets which are very delicate and should not be handled.

2- Each leaf therefore should be picked and transferred using gilders tips. Stroke the brush on the base of the neck or the forehead to "electrify" it so that when it is brought near to the edge of the leaf, the leaf itself is "attracted". Place it on the cushion to cut it and then pick it up again with the gilders tips, slowly and delicately, since the

least breath of air will blow it away. Then apply it to the surface to be silvered.

3- Gently work over it with an ox bristle brush to fix the leaf to the surface.

4- If the final surface is treated with several coats of gum lacquer, it will take on a golden appearance.

The bain marie used to prepare rabbit skin glue.

1

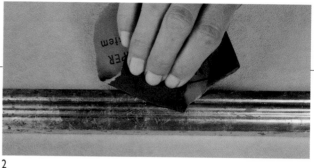

2

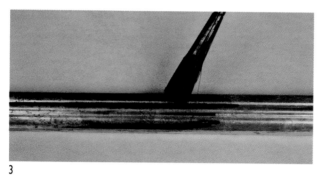

3

3a

Finishing

Having completed the gilding process the decoration should be protected. Varnishing is essential for dressed gilding but can be omitted for sized gilding which is itself quite resistant.

1- Because of its warm yellow colouring, imitation gold leaf is best treated with one or two coats of slightly diluted turpentine-based varnish; for silvering, it is best to use a completely transparent water-based varnish.

2- If the silvering is made on a dressed surface, always be very careful when applying the first coat of protective water-based varnish: there is the risk of spoiling all your efforts! If the object is to be antiquated, glass-paper lightly with paper n. 400 or 600 over the parts subject to wear before varnishing.

3 & 3a- Having applied the varnish, the antiquating patina can be brushed on; blend afterwards with a small rag (3a), leaving more product in the grooves.

A small gypsum stucco (above) was gilded and then antiquated.

GLOSSARY

Abrasive paper.
A siliconed paper used with water for surface polishing.

Acetate. A transparent or semi-transparent film used to prepare stencil templates.

Acrylic glue.
An acrylic bonding agent.

Acrylic paint. A fast-drying, water-based paint. Once dry, it is insoluble.

Antiquating.
A technique which imitates the effects of time in a recent decoration.

Arabesque.
An interweaved and fluent style of linear decoration.

Baroque. An artistic style developed in the 16th century which emphasizes emotional response through a combination of colour and movement.

Base coat. A substance applied to a surface to be decorated to make it less absorbent and easier to decorate.

Bolus. A coloured clay which, when mixed with rabbit skin glue, is sometimes applied to gypsum before gilding or silvering.

Bonding agent. Any liquid substance mixed with powder pigments to form a paint or dye.

Bordering. A finishing technique used to draw lines and borders around a surface to highlight its form.

Burnishing.
A technique used to hone and polish a metal object or surface.

Combs. Plastic or wooden toothed instruments originally intended for

reproducing sea effects. Can also be made from stiff card.

Copy paper. Used to copy a design from a sheet of paper and transfer it to another surface.

Cornice. A frame placed between the wall and the ceiling. Once manufactured on-site, frames are pre-fabricated today.

Country. Decoration characterized by simple and repetitive motifs.

Découpage.
Decoration of a surface using paper cuttings.

Dilutant. A liquid used to dilute lacquers. Turpentine and oil of turpentine are dilutants for oily lacquers.

Diluting (watering down). Diluting dyes and paints to

make them more transparent.

Drying agents.
Products which accelerate the drying of oil-based preparations.

Encaustic. Mural decoration made using pigments mixed with hot wax.

Festoon. Ornamental element usually comprising draped floral branches.

Filler. A transparent or matt preparation used to protect wood by filling pores.

Fixer. A substance used to stabilize paints, colours and dyes. The term is also used to describe a preparation which isolates masonry surfaces, forming an ideal base for other coatings.

Flogger brush.
A rough-tipped mane

brush used to paint stripes.

Framing. Marking out a section of a cornice in stucco or wood.

Fresco. A wall-painting technique involving paints diluted in water applied to a base of fresh plaster.

Gilding. Technique of applying gold leaf to a variety of surfaces such as picture frames.

Gilding brush. A brush with bristles enclosed between two thin pieces of card used to pick up gold leaf for water-based gilding.

Gilding cushion. A small cushion or pad used in gilding to support and protect the gold leaf, which is extremely delicate.

Glass-paper. Paper with glass granules or powder coating used to polish surfaces.

Gold leaf. Leaves of extremely thin gold (0.0001) using in gilding.

Goldsmith's knife. A finely balanced knife used to cut gold leaf.

Graphite paper. Transfer paper with a graphite powder additive used in place of carbon paper for an indelible result.

Grisaille. Monochrome decorative painting reproducing architectural or sculptural elements. Often used in trompe l'oeil; normally used in various shades of grey, red and "terracotta", it can equally be used with any other colour.

Grotesque. Mural decorations involving fantasy figures and scrolls.

Gum lacquer. A paint made from the resin secreted by particular kinds of ladybird.

Gypsum (chalk). A white powder; when mixed with animal glue and applied in several layers, it forms an extremely smooth surface.

Highlight. The most luminous part of an object, often a reflection or the point receiving the most direct light.

Imitation marble. A decorative technique used with a variety of materials, such as wood or masonry, to simulate the appearance of marble.

Inset panel. A panel recessed between the load-bearing elements of doors and hatches such as uprights and partitions.

Lacquer. A substance which, when applied to a decoration, forms a transparent protective film. Lacquers can be matt, semi-matt, shiny and water- or oil-based.

Lacquering. A technique which imitates the very particular brightness or shine of Chinese or Japanese lacquer-finishing.

Lilly bristle brush. Brush used especially to create imitation wood effects.

Linseed oil. Yellowish vegetable oil; it is one of the main ingredients in ageing patinas.

Luminosity. A term used to indicate the quantity of white in a colour, i.e. the lightness or darkness of the colour in question. Different colours may therefore have the same luminosity.

Manilla paper. An oiled paper used to make stencil templates.

Motif. A decorative element used repeatedly in a composition or drawing.

Mural. A wall painting.

Natural sponge. A marine sponge often used not only in sponging techniques to apply or remove product, but also for achieving marble effects and in free-hand drawing.

Neo-Gothic. An architectural style of the 19th century characterized by a return in modern form to the architecture typical of the Mediaeval Gothic period.

Perforated paper. A patterned card with holes used to transfer a design onto the surface to be decorated.

Perspective. The representation of a three-dimensional space on a flat surface. Aerial perspective creates the illusion of space and receding lines through the use of lights, shades and softened, cool colours for distant objects; linear perspective creates an idea of space on a flat surface through converging lines and vanishing points.

Pigment. A dye used to prepare paints.

Plumb-line. A thin cord with a weight at

the end used to check vertical straight lines.

Preliminary drawing (draft). Usually a pencil drawing transferred using graphite paper onto the surface to be decorated before colouring.

Primary colours. Colours which, when variously mixed, produce all other colours. Primary colours are red, yellow and blue. Various combinations create the secondary colours.

Primer (base coat). The first coat in painting used in the majority of decorative techniques.

Pure wax. Beeswax used by decorators to protect and polish surface finishes.

Rabbit skin glue. Glue prepared from animal cartilage, used in gilding to prepare the gypsum.

Register marks. Marks indicating the alignment of masks/ templates/stencils when more than one colour is used or if a repetitive motif is applied to a cornice.

Rococo. A decorative style which originated in France in the early 18th century, characterized by fluent forms and curves and delicate ornamentation.

Sable brush. A high quality fine art brush.

Sealing primer. Matt white oil paint applied to surfaces when preparing bases for special kinds of decoration.

Secondary colours. Colours produced by mixing two primary colours.

Silvering. The application of silver leaf to a pre-prepared surface.

Size. An oil used as an adhesive with gold leaf. Also available commercially in versions having different drying times.

Spirit-level. A glass tube partly filled with alcohol; the central position of the air bubble indicates the horizontal.

Spirits of turpentine (thinners). A mineral dilutant used as a solvent to clean brushes and dilute oily lacquers.

Squaring. A method by which a grid is drawn to enlarge or reduce an image or transfer it on to a wall or floor.

Steel wool. An abrasive comprising very fine threads of steel available in a variety of thicknesses. Also known as steel pads.

Stencils. A decorative technique in which the decoration is applied through a template (stencil), paper tape mask, a sheet of acetate or other material in which an outline has been cut, the remaining parts of which protect the areas which are not to be decorated.

Stub brush. A brush with rounded hog bristles used in a variety of decorative techniques and for "spotting".

Stucco. A finishing material for walls or wooden surfaces used to fill small pores or cracks.

Support (base). Canvas, paper, wood or other surfaces used in decorative work.

Template. A flat, cut-out model used as a base for difficult or complex designs.

Trompe l'oeil. A painting intended to "trick the eye" of the observer by presenting an apparently three-dimensional scene or object.

Truncated brush. A brush with short bristles used to transfer very small amounts of paint.

Turpentine. A high quality resin-based dilutant used to dilute oily lacquers or clean brushes.

Vanishing point. The point on the horizon where two parallel lines seem to meet.

Veiling. Working a very dilute colour over a surface which has already been decorated; this achieves a very transparent coating, similar to a veil.

Water-painting. Painting with water-based paints.

The works presented in this book were developed by the founding partners, students and members of the Academy.
Special acknowledgements to:
Emanuale Bongianni and Daniela Urbinati, pages 106, 160, 168, 169:
Mariange Grabau, pages 64, 90, 133;
Susanna Montagna and Federica Tedesco, pages 73, 111, 113;
Piero Pietracci, page 146;
Marisa Rossi, pages 44, 68, 135.